THE PSYCHOLOGY OF RETIREMENT

How can you make the most of retirement? How should you plan for retirement? What are the challenges of retirement and how can they be dealt with?

The Psychology of Retirement looks at this life stage as a journey that involves challenges, opportunities, setbacks, periods of disenchantment and, often, exciting new beginnings. Taking a positive approach, the book explores how retirement provides opportunities to cultivate new friendships, interests and hobbies, consolidate and renegotiate long-held ones, and even re-invent oneself in a post-work environment. It also emphasizes the value of pre-retirement planning, and the importance of establishing new goals and purposes.

Retirement can be a period of significant psychological growth and development and The Psychology of Retirement shows how it can herald the beginning of a vibrant and active stage of life.

Emeritus Professor **Doreen Rosenthal** and Emeritus Professor **Susan Moore** are social researchers and retired academics who write extensively for both academic and non-academic audiences. They have jointly authored books on adolescence, sexuality, grandparenting, and retirement. They take their own advice about retirement, aiming to stay mentally, physically and socially active.

THE PSYCHOLOGY OF EVERYTHING

The Psychology of Everything is a series of books which debunk the myths and pseudo-science surrounding some of life's biggest questions.

The series explores the hidden psychological factors that drive us, from our sub-conscious desires and aversions, to the innate social instincts handed to us across the generations. Accessible, informative, and always intriguing, each book is written by an expert in the field, examining how research-based knowledge compares with popular wisdom, and illustrating the potential of psychology to enrich our understanding of humanity and modern life.

Applying a psychological lens to an array of topics and contemporary concerns – from sex to addiction to conspiracy theories – The Psychology of Everything will make you look at everything in a new way.

Titles in the series:

For further information about this series please visit:
www.thepsychologyofeverything.co.uk

THE PSYCHOLOGY OF RETIREMENT

DOREEN ROSENTHAL AND SUSAN MOORE

Routledge
Taylor & Francis Group

LONDON AND NEW YORK

First published 2019
by Routledge
2 Park Square, Milton Park, Abingdon, Oxon OX14 4RN

and by Routledge
711 Third Avenue, New York, NY 10017

Routledge is an imprint of the Taylor & Francis Group, an informa business

British Library Cataloguing-in-Publication Data
A catalogue record for this book is available from the British Library

Library of Congress Cataloging-in-Publication Data
A catalog record for this book has been requested

ISBN: 978-0-8153-4707-1 (hbk)
ISBN: 978-0-8153-4708-8 (pbk)
ISBN: 978-1-351-16988-2 (ebk)

Typeset in Joanna
by Apex CoVantage, LLC

Printed and bound by CPI Group (UK) Ltd, Croydon, CR0 4Y*

CONTENTS

ACKNOWLEDGEMENTS

We would like to thank our colleagues and institutions (the Centre for Women's Health, Gender and Society, Melbourne School of Population Health at The University of Melbourne and the Department of Psychological Sciences, Faculty of Health, Arts and Design at Swinburne University of Technology) for providing the resources that enabled us to complete this book. Thanks also to research assistants Alex Poll and Kerrie Shandley who assisted us with their careful work. Special acknowledgement and thanks are due to the women and men who generously gave their time and considered thoughts as part of our studies.

We thank our publisher for continuing support and encouragement. Finally, our thanks once again to Ian and David who sustain us always.

1

THE NEW RETIREMENT

GREY POWER

Are you about to retire, or have you done so already? Here's a thought experiment. If you are able, compare yourself with your father, mother, grandfather and grandmother when (or if) they retired. Are you younger or older? Fitter and healthier, or not? Better or worse off financially? As far as you know, how do your expectations about retirement, quality and length of life compare with those of your parents and grandparents? Were your mother or grandmother in the paid workforce and thus eligible to 'retire' or did they continue with their household and caring roles long past retirement age?

Of course, everyone will have different memories, but a common pattern for baby boomers is to recall their fathers retiring and living only a few years longer, while their mothers, homemakers for most of their adult lives, spent many years as widows. A large percentage of baby boomers may not have known their grandparents, given the typical lifespans of that earlier generation. Indeed, life expectancy at birth for those born in the 1890s was around 44 for men and 48 for women, increasing for those born in the early 1920s to 55.6 for men and 59.6 for women.[1] Those who made it to 'retirement age' in either of these generations were therefore the lucky ones. According to the

Office for National Statistics, these days life expectancy at birth in the UK is 79.1 years for men and 82.5 years for women.[2] It has increased by eight years for men and six years for women since the early 1980s. For those who avoid an early death and reach retirement age, lifespans are likely to be even longer. In 2013–2015, a 65-year-old man in the UK had, on average, a further 18.5 years of life remaining (bringing him to 83.5 years) and a woman 20.9 years (bringing her to nearly 86 years). Similar statistics characterise other English-speaking nations such as the US, Australia, Canada and New Zealand, as well as many European countries.

Two clear trends are evident in these statistics, and they apply not only in developed nations but also across the world. First, we are living longer – generally many years post the typical retirement ages of between 60 and 65 years. Second, there is a gap between male and female lifespans, one that varies between countries and eras. Currently it is between three and five years in the developed world, a gap that is narrowing (although not as quickly as predicted). Our increased lifespans are accompanied by better health and fitness. Improvements in living conditions, diet and medical care, as well as greater public understanding of healthy lifestyles have contributed to this increase.

There are some important implications of all these demographic facts. First, retirement can no longer be considered as a short rest before inevitable illness and death; it can extend 20 or 30 years, up to a third of our whole lifespan. It is a new life stage, part of our psychological development. Like all life stages, it involves transitions, adjustments, opportunities for psychological growth and traps for the unwary. We need to find things to do and ways to live in our retirement years, ways that are meaningful and satisfying.

Second, the gender gap in life expectancy, coupled with the fact that most women partner with somewhat older men, means that the likelihood of women outliving their partners by 5 to 10 years (in some cases much longer) is high. Many women, perhaps the majority, will spend their final years of life as singles. Examination of the final stage of life in which ageing concerns become most prominent is not the major focus of this book, however it is worth noting the role of both close families and female friendships in providing support during these older years. Certainly during the earlier stages of retirement, there is opportunity to strengthen and nurture such ties. This is likely to be rewarding during the here-and-now of active retirement, as well as contributing to a bulwark of support as the ageing process runs its inevitable course.

Finally, as the world population ages, retirees are becoming an increasingly large cohort. The baby boomer generation has reached their 60s and 70s. They are retiring 'en masse', drawing on their superannuation, government pensions and health care resources. Does this mean that retirees will become a drain on the economies of nations? Or will their capacity to contribute – for example as consumers and investors, as carers of grandchildren and elderly relatives, as family mentors and supports – value add to society in ways that override the outcomes of non-participation in the paid workforce? Only time will tell, but it is clear that governments are worried about the economic effects of this large cohort, with many countries increasing the age at which social service and government pensions become available.[3] Of course, as seniors remain longer in paid employment, there will be a series of social knock-on effects, some intended, some unintended. Examples, to name just a few, include effects on the labour market, on the 'volunteer workforce', and on the childcare, travel and housing industries.

By way of balance, we should be aware that another feature of the expanding population of retirees is that this group forms a large voting bloc. Thus there is pressure on governments to provide services for retired seniors, to listen to complaints and take note of suggestions. Retirees have power!

WHAT DO WE MEAN BY RETIREMENT?

Retirement is the new promotion.[4]

A dictionary definition of 'retire' is to 'leave one's job and cease to work, typically on reaching the normal age for leaving service'. That is certainly the traditional notion of retirement. You have a pleasant morning tea with fellow workers, they present you with a gold watch or (more likely) a bunch of flowers and off you go to your 'pensioned leisure', to play golf, do some fishing or bake scones. Shakespeare put these words into the mouth of the ageing King Lear as he expressed his readiness to retire:

> . . . and tis our fast intent
> To shake all cares and business from our age,
> Conferring them on younger strengths, while we
> Unburdened crawl towards death.

Simple, brutal and inaccurate. We don't need 10 or 20 years to plan for death. There's another life stage to be prepared for and live through, more maturing and psychological work to be done, more experiences and fun to be had. Newly retired people are recognising this change, as we found through the comments they made in one of our studies.[5] Many talked about new beginnings, rather than endings. Although all self-defined as retired, some felt uncomfortable about the application of this word to the active ways they were engaging with life.

> I see retirement as an opportunity to reinvent oneself.

> What is retirement? I have three volunteer workplaces, several elderly relatives and a grandchild to care for, a home and garden to keep, gym classes and more activities on offer than can be managed. What is quiet and retired about that?

> I didn't RETIRE, I simply stopped working in traditional sense. I did not stop working completely. The word 'RETIRE' here, implies that you leave one life for another.

Those researching retirement, like retirees themselves, can struggle with defining what it actually is. In an important review of the psychological literature, Wang and Shi (2004) point out how researchers have used many different definitions, including career cessation, reduced work effort, being in receipt of a pension or social security benefit, self-report or having reached a certain age.[6] There are many ambiguities in these attempts. 'Career cessation', for example, can involve retiring from a long-term career and beginning another. People in our studies talked about retiring for a second or even a third time. As well, it can be difficult to pinpoint just when 'cessation' occurs if an individual moves from full-time to part-time to casual work modes.

Age is not a clear indicator of retirement status. Some people never retire, particularly if they are self-employed. In most developed countries, a compulsory retiring age no longer exists except for a few specific occupations, usually those considered dangerous or requiring a high degree of mental or physical acuity, such as pilot, judge or military personnel. The major constraints against retiring 'late' (say in your 70s or 80s) mostly concern your health, your personal preferences, and the availability of work and your enjoyment of it.

Barriers against retiring 'early' (say, in your 50s) generally reduce to personal preference and the availability of finances. Access to government pensions is usually not possible until a specific age has been reached. In most Western countries, this entitlement age is between 60 and 65 years, but it is gradually rising as the world population ages and there are so many more retired people to be funded. Even drawing on your own retirement pension savings can attract economic penalties such as increased taxation if this occurs before a certain age.

Being on a government or superannuation pension does not necessarily indicate that you have retired, with many individuals working to supplement their pension incomes or simply for the pleasure of it. Some researchers have defined a retired person as one whose pension payments exceed the amount they earn in paid employment, but even a definition as seemingly objective as this does not necessarily align with people's self-reports.

Weiss (2005) suggested that retirement can be defined in three general ways. An *economic* definition relates to when an older person has ceased paid work; a *sociological* definition relates to when someone no longer works and has reached an age where this is socially acceptable; a *psychological* definition is when a person self-identifies as retired.[7] This book is directed at those who self-define as retired or preparing to retire, and although we discuss research that uses other definitions of retirement, it is a self-report approach that we prefer.

The slogan at the beginning of this section, presenting retirement as a kind of promotion, puts a new slant on this life stage, one that is very different from that encompassed in the King Lear quotation. Describing retirement as a 'promotion' reminds us of the potential for this stage to be positive, active and full of challenges, whichever way it is defined.

RETIREMENT REASONS, STYLES AND TYPES

REASONS

Ideally, your retirement date will be chosen and planned for well ahead of time. Unfortunately, in the real world, such choice is not always possible. Workers in their 50s and 60s can be made redundant and find it difficult or even impossible to find other work. Some feel constrained to retire because of ill health, the care needs of others, job stress or problems dealing with changes in the workplace, such as the introduction of new technologies.

Retirement wellbeing and ease of coping with this life stage are strongly related to reasons for retiring.[8] In our research, those made redundant were significantly less satisfied with their finances, their social life, their level of physical activity, their standard of living and their life in general than those who left work voluntarily. They also rated themselves as significantly less financially secure than voluntary retirees, no doubt because they had a shorter length of time to plan for and accumulate savings and pension credits.

Research from all over the world indicates that, not surprisingly, men and women who are able to choose the time and circumstances of their retirement fare better in terms of retirement outcomes. Ill health, family pressures and work organisational reasons for finishing work can all impact not only on finances but on future mental and physical wellbeing and quality of relationships. Of course, these are trends only. Many people 'bounce back' from a redundancy, find that life is less stressful in retirement and/or are able, with greater rest and relaxation, to improve their health status post-work. Some examples from our research participants illustrate this kind of resilience.

> When I was made redundant, I decided to take it. I did not want to be deployed to another district or state. It was an enormously hard decision to make and be comfortable with. . . . That sounds negative, but now I'm loving not having to work in such a stressful field of employment.

> I was very lucky that I was able to retire when I was made redundant, as I was then able to really support my parents in their last couple of years. My younger sisters were still very much working and could not take time to do this. They were very grateful I was managing it all. I was very glad I could do it.

STYLES

There are at least three different styles of retirement.[9] First is the traditional 'cold turkey' approach, where paid work ceases altogether. One day you are a worker, next day a retiree with time to fill. Men and women who choose (or fall into) this approach do not necessarily fit the 'gone fishing' stereotype of spending their days in lazy leisure activities; many participate in volunteer work, care for grandchildren, involve themselves in clubs, play competitive sports, travel, garden, study, do home renovations . . . the list is endless. For this group there will be a likely fading of former occupational interests, links with past workplaces and identification as a 'worker'. Different self-definitions will emerge or strengthen, such as 'volunteer', 'grandparent', 'craftsperson' or 'golfer'. The risks for this group are loneliness, boredom and social isolation. Without planning and organisation, time can hang heavy.

A second retirement style is the transitional approach, where people gradually withdraw from the workforce through part-time or casual work. There may be no clear-cut moment when transitionals define themselves as 'retired', so their identification as a worker remains for a longer time than for the 'cold turkey' retirees. Professionals, academics and people running their own businesses often choose this form of gradual retirement where they ease out of paid work lives, taking time to try out and experiment with non-work interests and activities. One academic put it this way:

> I wound down over about five years, going from full-time to four days a week, then three days, then two. This way I was able to complete projects at work and hand over some of my responsibilities gradually. It also meant that over those five years I had a clear day each week to devote to my two pre-school grandchildren, but I also had excuses not to be too over committed to baby-sitting!

Such a model of gradual retirement has many advantages for those who enjoy their work but find that a full-time commitment becomes stressful as ageing proceeds and the recognition that life is finite becomes more powerful. A risk can be the difficulty of weaning yourself away from your worker identity and so delaying desired activities such as travel or relationship strengthening for too long. If you've always wanted to walk from Land's End to John O'Groats, probably better to try it at 60 than at 80. If you want to bond more strongly with your grandchildren, best not wait until they are teenagers or young adults.

The third retirement style has been labelled 'transformative'. Retirees in this group start on new projects (or even careers) that fill a good proportion of their day and provide a new identity, a new self-description. Sometimes these come about as a fulfilment of life-long dream. An example would be the person who always wanted to express their creative side but had neither the time nor the financial flexibility to do so during their middle years. On retirement, this retiree takes art lessons, goes on painting tours, and sets up exhibitions. The former accountant or math teacher is now an artist.

Transformative retirement may occur when individuals experiment and search for new ways to fill their time, and a particular interest or activity becomes a new passion. Sometimes it is simply serendipity – a chance meeting or an article in a newspaper set off a chain of events that culminate in a new career – paid or unpaid – for the retiree. Some examples:

> I didn't expect that a hobby I took up in retirement (decoupage) would provide me with the skill to set up my own little cottage industry. I worked hard at this, simply because I enjoyed it very much, and eventually made enough money at local craft markets to travel overseas for 2 two- and three-month holidays.

> I didn't expect my husband and I would start a charity. It has evolved far beyond our original vision and we are now engaged in succession planning.

One of the issues facing the transformative retiree is that they may find themselves needing to retire more than once! Indeed, these different ways of retiring are not mutually exclusive. A person might retire completely from their long-term career, spend a year or two engaged in leisure and domestic activities, then return to the same or a different workplace, either full time or part time. So long as a retiree's health is good and jobs are available, there is flexibility. In fact, writers now discuss the value of 'unretirement' as an excellent financial strategy, especially for those who took early retirement and may find their funds dwindling more quickly than they expected.

TYPES

Counselling psychologist Nancy Schlossberg developed a six-category retiree typology, focussing on psychological and behavioural characteristics rather than work patterns.[10] 'Continuers' maintained their pre-retirement interests and skills, using them in further work, volunteer or hobby situations. 'Adventurers' began entirely new pursuits after retirement, often taking up activities they had not had time for during their working years, such as travel or artistic endeavours. 'Searchers' experimented with a range of new activities, exploring many interests through trial and error. Less purposeful were the 'Easy Gliders', who enjoyed the freedom and flexibility of letting each day unfold but without any fixed goals, and the 'Retreaters', who disengaged from many former pursuits, wanting to wind down and reduce life stress. 'Involved Spectators' were also less active than Continuers, Adventurers and Searchers, but while they shared some characteristics of Retreaters, they did maintain a high level of interest in the world around them. A retiree's type may be in part associated with personality characteristics, but as Schlossbeg points out, it is also likely to be dependent on many other factors such as age of retirement, mental and physical health and financial and family circumstances. One's 'type' may also change as retirement (and age) progress; these should not be considered as fixed categories.

LOSS OF THE WORK ROLE

> Work banishes those three evils: boredom, vice and poverty.[11]

Why do lifespan psychologists consider retirement as an adjustment, a life change that requires a degree of coping and adaptation? Doesn't everyone want to give up work, relax and do as they please? What's the problem here? Why all the fuss?

It seems that work – especially work you love – is fulfiling in more ways than just providing a pay packet. Of course we work to earn a living, but even jobs you don't particularly enjoy can have positive influences on your lifestyle. One famous study of unemployment, conducted in 1933 but still relevant today, delineated these 'latent' (or less obvious) functions of employment.[12] Marie Jahoda and her colleagues became participant observers of life in the Austrian village of Marienthal, where a key industry, employing most of the town, had recently closed down. Most in the community were out of work. The resultant apathy, depression and sense of hopelessness experienced by so many of the community went beyond the deprivations associated with financial hardship. Although being unemployed and retired are not the same, they share the requirement that you need to take active steps to restructure your time once work no longer fills your days.

In fact, this classic research study found that one of the major 'latent' functions of work was that it helps us to structure our time. We have a reason to get up at a certain hour each morning, a reason to stay groomed, fit and alert. We have the reward of a limited amount of leisure time to look forward to when the workday is over. The unemployed can find they have too much free time; they feel bored and unmotivated without the structure that their employment once provided. When we asked retirees what they missed most about work, a significant number commented on this aspect.

> I miss the structure of a workplace where your work responsibilities and activities are clear.

> Perhaps the only thing [I miss] is that there was a structure to those days that I was working. Now I have had to ensure that my days are structured so that I do not bludge around.

Maintenance of social contact is another key latent function of work. There are people to chat with in most workplaces, although interestingly, the increasingly common phenomenon of 'working from home' may mean that home-based workers need to resolve issues of social isolation well before their retirement years. Nevertheless, in workplaces where one meets fellow workers or customers on a daily basis, there is a social aspect to the day. Experiences and goals can be shared. Interactions with colleagues and workplace friends can be enriching, interesting and broadening, giving the worker food for thought and conversational topics to share at home and with friends and family. There is no need to make special arrangements to set up workplace socialisation; it occurs as a natural part of the working day. One risk for retirees is social isolation and loneliness, unless a conscious effort is made to develop and maintain engagement with other people. We discuss this important consequence of retirement in Chapter 5.

Retirees told us that social contact was one of the aspects of work they missed most, especially in early retirement before they had engaged with new social groups.

> I miss the companionship of working in a team. Miss some of the social connections that I once enjoyed.

> I initially missed being part of a 'team' but as time goes on, I have replaced my work team with many other social 'teams' and no longer miss the work team environment.

A third latent function of work is a sense of collective purpose (also alluded to in some of the quotes above). Being part of a work team contributes to feelings of being useful and needed and contributing to communal goals. These may be goals related to altruism (helping others), quality (making beautiful or functional items), production (improving last month's sales figures), competition (becoming the most profitable division) or some other work values or combination of values. Retirees can re-establish such a sense of collective purpose in volunteer or creative work, or even in family projects, but to do so requires self-motivation and self-directedness that can be difficult to sustain. Retirees put it this way:

> I miss the clear purpose of each day and the plans and tasks that were laid out before me.

> [I miss] spending time each day working on projects that benefited the community and influenced how peopled lived. This provided a sense of having a broader purpose in life.

Another function of work – even the mere fact of being employed – is that it provides people with a certain status in life, an identity that is readily summed up in a few words – 'I'm a chemist' or 'I'm a car salesman'. This is particularly true of professional and skilled labour. The unemployed, and to some extent retirees, can feel stigmatised and that they are somehow of lower worth. One retired blogger, Syd, calls this 'the cocktail party dilemma'.[13] How do you answer the question about your working life that inevitably arises when you meet a new person? Syd discusses this and writes about his fear of being no longer interesting to others:

> After I retired, I found that telling people I was retired didn't have the same effect of propelling the conversation forward. . . . Perhaps some people thought 'retired' was a euphemism for out of work. . . . Other people responded by asking what I did all day, usually accompanied with the assertion that they would die of boredom if they retired. And to be fair, when you list out what you can recall that you actually 'do' all day, it does sound kind of boring.

Retired women we interviewed commented along the same lines.

> I miss the recognition and status.

> I miss the identity. Who am I without a business card?

Finally, jobs keep us active both mentally and physically. They keep us interacting with the world out there, exercising the mind and the body. The risk for retirees is in becoming a couch potato, unstimulated, unmotivated and uninteresting. Certainly retirement is an opportunity to take it easier, to enjoy rest and relaxation, but retirees also need interests and activities that excite, inspire, engage and connect them with others. While some will retire with interests they cannot wait to pursue, others – especially the workaholic – may need time and effort to find new passions that provide both purpose and enjoyment.

One retiree summed up these work functions in her explanation of what she missed most about her working life.

> [I miss] the interaction with colleagues, a structure for the working week, the feeling that you are doing something worthwhile and interesting, learning new skills and maintaining existing skills, participating and cooperating with team and fellow workers on shared projects, belonging to something.

To summarise then, a major psychosocial challenge for retirees is to find new activities and ways of thinking to substitute for the functions that work once fulfiled in their lives. Throughout this book we discuss these in more detail as well as more and less successful approaches to making this transition.

THIS BOOK

In this book we follow the journey of today's retirees, through planning and decision-making, expectations, early experiences, pleasures and disappointments. Factors influencing successful and unsuccessful coping with this life stage are considered, with particular emphasis on financial issues, health maintenance, social connectedness and renegotiating identity in the retirement years. We describe the retirement experiences of both men and women, exploring similarities and differences in their resources and coping styles. We deal with questions of how successful retirement can be facilitated, and use current research to attempt to answer questions such as 'When is the best time to retire?'; 'How can I plan for retirement?'; and 'What are the pitfalls?'

One key issue in researching the retirement experience is that outcomes are readily conflated with the effects of ageing. If retired people show changes in their health status, for example, is this a function of their retirement or is it because this group is experiencing ageing effects? A few careful studies have been able to separate out these effects (to some extent) either statistically or through comparing workers and retirees matched on age and other important variables like socio-economic status. There is an extended discussion of this issue in our chapter on health and retirement, but it is one to keep in mind as you proceed. In a sense, it is not possible to completely separate the effects of retiring from the effects of ageing, as they occur together.

This book, *Psychology of Retirement*, draws on contemporary qualitative and quantitative psychological research, positioning this research within its social context. Throughout the book we draw on our own research with seniors groups, particularly a large-scale survey of retired Australian women, published works on grandmothers and grandfathers, and feedback from the men and women we meet during our many presentations to retiree groups. We quote liberally from these sources to illustrate and expand on findings from the social science literature.

2

THE JOURNEY
TRANSITIONING FROM WORKER TO RETIREE

The process of retiring takes us on a psychological journey as we move from one life stage to another. The time it takes to make the physical transition to retirement – that is, to leave the workplace behind – will not necessarily correspond to the time it takes for the psychological journey. We are all different. Some who retire literally overnight will move seamlessly into planned activities, new roles and greater involvement in already existing non-work roles such as grand-parenting. Others will find themselves overwhelmed by the lack of structure in their lives and will take more time to adjust. For some, gradual retirement will assist adaptation to new roles; for others it might simply delay this process, stretching it out over a longer time frame.

Life transitions like retirement are developmental changes that involve discontinuities with previous life events. Discontinuities that occur quickly and are irreversible can be difficult to cope with, even when they are benign. Becoming a parent for the first time is an example of a sudden, irreversible life transition. While it may be wonderful and joyous, there will be ups and downs, heightened emotions and feelings of being overwhelmed. With time, new parents learn to adjust their lifestyles and expectations to create a new reality of 'family' instead of just 'couple'.

All transitions are like this, in that they require us to learn new ways of being and adjust to a different set of expectations and roles. When we retire, we move from a relatively predictable mode of existence into unknown territory. Do we still need to get up early and dress to impress? What tasks will we achieve and who will we talk to today? What is there to talk about anyway, without the focus on workplace issues and our former colleagues? These changes require emotional adjustment; they can be disorienting at best and depressing at worst. As well, our attitudes might need to change, especially if we have previously held negative stereotypes of retired people as 'past their use-by date'. Not the least of it, our sense of self will require cognitive restructuring. Who are we now, if not doctor, teacher, salesperson, administrator, taxi driver?

One writer, Cussen (2017), suggests there are six typical stages in the retirement journey.[1] These are planning (the pre-retirement phase), 'the big day' (farewells), the honeymoon period, disenchantment, re-orientation and re-establishing a routine. In this chapter, we expand on each of these in turn, keeping in mind that not all retirees will necessarily follow the same pathway or the same order of stages. It is possible that those who retire gradually over a period of years may work through their transition more gently. Not all retirees will experience a honeymoon period or a disenchantment phase. Those who retire for a second or even third time might have different experiences again. Forced redundancies and other pressures to retire are likely to make adjustment more difficult and its process lengthier than retirement occurring through free choice. Despite these caveats, many retirees will recognise their own experiences in Cussen's stages. Acknowledgement of their typicality may be a useful aid to self-understanding and provide guidance for those considering retirement in the future.

PLANNING

Imagining our own retirement is a precursor to planning for it. What were (or are) your thoughts about this life stage during your 20s, 30s and 40s? Perhaps you conflated stereotypes of retirement with stereotypes of ageing, writing off these years as ones of disengagement and infirmity. Perhaps you envisaged an endless holiday, a time when you could finally sleep in, read or play golf all day, answering to no one. More likely you never gave retirement a second thought, except to sometimes notice the retirement fund deductions in your pay packet.

But as people reach their 50s and 60s, thoughts about retirement become more salient. It is not uncommon for workers to begin mental preparation for this change, through talking to others, seeking information, considering when to leave, developing appropriate exit strategies, examining finances and thinking about activities and roles that might be part of a new post-work lifestyle. This is a healthy approach. Research is clear that planning assists adjustment and satisfaction with retirement. But it is not always easy to manage the headspace necessary for organising the future when the concerns of the present are pressing.

Financial planning, which we discuss in detail in Chapter 3, is particularly important, but unfortunately many people find this difficult, boring and anxiety arousing. One US study demonstrated that nearly half of a large sample of participants found it difficult to even think about, let alone plan, their retirement finances.[2] Very few of the workers surveyed had tried to calculate how much money they would need in retirement, or even understood how to go about doing this. Yet calculations of this sort are important in decisions about when might be the best time to retire. Delaying retirement even for a year or two can assist workers to pay off debts, increase savings and sometimes gain more generous access to social security benefits and government pensions. In the US study, women especially felt overwhelmed, confused and negative about financial planning, a task that many admitted to avoiding, even though they worried about it. Yet our studies and those of others show, not surprisingly, that those who make financial plans are more economically secure in retirement, a factor that is one of the strongest predictors of retirement adjustment and later life satisfaction.

But planning is not all about money. As one retiree told us:

> Having had the experience I think there is not enough mental preparation – I think it is like having a baby, you can read all about it, but until you experience it nothing you read makes sense.

Lifestyle planning – thinking about and arranging post-retirement activities, new roles and interests – is another important aspect of preparation for exit from the workforce. The move from structured time in the workforce to unstructured time in retirement can be a challenge. It may seem like a holiday at first, but after the first flush of freedom, time can hang heavy. Planning activities and setting some goals for the first few years of retirement are strategies likely to assist in alleviating the possibility of boredom or loss of purpose. You may need to experiment to find what you enjoy. What does seem important is to keep both mind and body active, and to maintain social contacts, issues we discuss further in several chapters of this book.

Retirees from our study had plenty of comments and advice about lifestyle planning.

> I planned my retirement with thought to ensure there were activities for Brain, Body and Soul.

> [If I had my time over] I'd devote more time to making a plan about what to do with all the extra time.

> [If I had my time over] I would have planned more activities. I got a bit of a shock when I first retired but quickly overcame lack of things to do. I found volunteering where I could use my brain and this is valued.

Of course, some people 'wing it' quite successfully, and others find their plans do not eventuate as circumstances change. Planning is a process, not a one-off activity. Flexibility is important as your world alters. Life events can turn plans on their head, as this retiree reminded us.

> I am circumspect about perfect plans. Life is not like that.

FAREWELLING THE WORKPLACE

Whether your disengagement from the workplace comprises a one-off celebration or a long goodbye, there is at least one study suggesting that marking the event with some kind of public ritual is beneficial.[3]

We celebrate other transitions such as 21st birthdays, weddings and baptisms. These events are a social statement of the importance of the life change and the desire that it be recognised and accepted by family and friends. There is an implicit expectation that support will be available if needed for the individual facing their new life status. In the case of retirement, a send-off provides an opportunity for the retiring worker to both be acknowledged by and to acknowledge co-workers. It presents a clear message to all that one stage of life is over and a new one is beginning.

Van den Bogaard's research showed that experiencing a retirement ritual was positively associated with post-retirement life satisfaction, particularly for those who perceived themselves as highly competent in their work. So it is worth considering ways to mark the ending of your paid work life, or of leaving a workplace where you have been employed for many years. Not so easy, of course, for those who do not have a specific workplace to leave, such as visiting tradespeople or those who work from their own homes. This is a group who tends to retire by gradually cutting down their hours. Even so, a social acknowledgement of the occasion when one decides to 'wind down' can assist both retirees and their friends and families to move to the next life stage.

HONEYMOON PHASE

The honeymoon phase is really about acknowledging that so many of the constraints and stresses that surrounded you as a worker have now been removed. It's a realisation that is usually (but not always) accompanied by positive emotions like relief and joy. When we asked retirees to name the best aspects of their new life stage, 'freedom!' was so often the response. This was sometimes expressed as freedom *to* – 'to do what I want when I want', 'to no longer have a regimented lifestyle', 'to have control of my day to day activities', or 'to be able to do whatever I like for the first time in my life'. Others focused on their new-found freedoms *from*, especially from work-related stresses, as in 'no one to tell me what to do', 'no more conflicts with employees', 'not having to look after other people any more', 'not being subjected to bullying bosses' and 'not having to conform to a rigid schedule at work'.

Another benefit felt keenly by the newly retired is having more time. For many, this extra time meant simply 'sleeping in' or 'not having to rush off in the morning'; for others it was an opportunity to engage in new (or old) activities and interests or spend more time with family. Volunteering, studying, sports, fitness classes and hobbies such as craft, reading, gardening and travel were all mentioned as pursuits our retirees now felt they had time for.

The increase in time and freedom (or self-directedness) brought about by retirement does not stay a novelty forever. Some retirees tire of it after a short time. One female participant in a US study put it this way:

> At first it felt like a vacation for about three weeks and then it didn't feel so good anymore. I was just floundering around like a fish out of water. So I started to plan my day just like I did when I was at work. And that felt good! I felt like I had a purpose.[4]

For those who have organised (or fallen into) immediate post-retirement activities or projects such as extended travel or home renovations, the feeling that they now have *too much time* on their hands, and *too much freedom*, is likely to be delayed. For some, of course, that feeling never arrives, but many retirees do come to an awareness that, for their lives to be meaningful and self-fulfiling over the next decade or three, they need to develop new roles, new interests and new ways to fill their days. Such awareness may be preceded by the next stage – disenchantment.

DISENCHANTMENT

> I must find something challenging to do! Crossword puzzles just don't cut it.[5]

> After longing for 'freedom' I got sick of that within 4 months. Is this all there is?

Cussen characterises this stage as the realisation that 'this is it', this is the rest of your life. It has the potential to be boring, to feel undirected and lacking in purpose. Retirees may experience apathy, lack of motivation, sadness and even depression as they confront a future in which ageing is the only certainty. Disenchantment with retirement can occur more than once, as various projects or activities are completed and the retiree wonders what to do next. Some people have called it the 'retirement blues'.

It may be helpful for retirees to understand that this phase of negative emotions is not uncommon – they are not alone or abnormal – it is part of the process of experiencing transition and change. As we age, these feelings may be particularly poignant as we recognise there is only so much time left, some of our life goals will never be fulfiled, and some of those we once had no longer seem important. Can we reframe our ambitions to make the most of each day left to us?

Relevant here is consideration of the work of developmental psychologist Erik Erikson, who wrote about how psychosocial maturity is something that grows and develops through different stages of life. At each life stage, he postulated a developmental 'crisis' to be worked through on the path to becoming a fully functioning adult. Resolution of each crisis may involve emotional upheavals and psychological costs. It's not only adolescents who experience existential angst, get moody and worry about what life has in store for them and how they will cope. Such feelings occur throughout life, particularly at periods of change.

For those at mid-life and beyond, Erikson emphasised the importance of developing a sense of generativity.[6] A generative person is one who makes contributions to society and future generations rather than focussing only on self-related concerns. Parenting is the usual – but not the only – path by which people make these contributions. Work too can contribute through one's productive efforts and through mentoring others. In Erikson's theory, the opposite of becoming generative is 'stagnation' – failure to find ways to contribute. Those who do not develop their sense of generativity feel disconnected from their community and from society in general; they may be self-absorbed, for example with the complaints of ageing or the need to appear young. The 'disenchantment' phase of retirement may be viewed as part of the struggle to move from this self-absorbed state to more mature fulfilment.

In retirement, some are able to find generative fulfilment through grandchildren, but this path is not open to all. Retirement has the potential to lead to exacerbation of the generativity 'crisis' unless significant activities and goals can be substituted for those provided in the work environment. This re-orientation of lifestyle is discussed below.

RE-ORIENTATION: BUILDING A NEW IDENTITY

Cussen says this is the stage where retirees ask questions like 'Who am I, now?' 'What is my purpose at this point?' and 'Am I still useful in some capacity?' Erikson might have phrased it as 'How can I justify my existence? or 'How can I contribute?' Dealing with such issues can be difficult and is likely to involve experimentation, setbacks and renegotiations. For example, expectations that you will spend significant time with grandchildren may not be realised, intentions to volunteer may be difficult to implement, or plans to travel may not come to fruition. You may face unexpected challenges like illness or death of a partner. However, experimentation with new and different activities, involvement with different kinds of organisations and meeting new people should be – and usually is – rewarding and fun. Over time, most retirees find new roles they enjoy, and new, satisfying ways to fill their days. Others do not achieve this resolution and find themselves discontented, playing out the role of grumpy old man or woman. In Chapter 6, we discuss in more detail the challenges of re-shaping one's identity in the retirement years, particularly among those who have always been heavily committed to the workforce.

ROUTINE: MOVING ON

Life changes, as we have seen, are often followed by disorientation, mood swings, experimentation and setbacks. Eventually, we adapt to a new state of being. For some retirees, this adaptation comes swiftly and joyfully.

> It's better [than I expected]. I liked being a busy young thing and now I'm enjoying being a slow old thing.

> I am doing things I have meant to do for years! I organised a street party last January, such a hit and will repeat next summer! I have a VERY firm belief, retirement is what YOU make it, and I just LOVE having the freedom and choice each day. Love it.

For others, it can take longer and require adjustments to unforeseen circumstances.

> My retirement was earlier than I'd planned. My husband is still working for financial reasons so I sometimes feel I am marking time until we can do the travelling things together.

> I had been a workaholic and was surprised that I did not miss working very much at all. Overall, retirement is better than expected. However, I must admit that initially I replaced paid work with a heavy dose of volunteer work, which I have now eased back on, and have finally, 10 years after retirement, achieved a better work/life balance for the first time in my life!

Over time, most retirees develop a new, non-work identity. New routines, different social worlds and re-imagined goals are established. Many describe these years as the best of their lives. One factor affecting successful adaptation to retirement is choosing the 'best' time to go. In the next section, we consider a range of variables that influence this decision.

WHEN IS THE BEST TIME TO RETIRE?[7]

WHEN YOU CHOOSE

The best time to go depends on many different factors but, as we saw in Chapter 1, one of the strongest predictors of retirement satisfaction is being able to make that choice on your own terms. An unexpected redundancy, as well as reducing your opportunity to make adequate financial and lifestyle plans for retirement, can be experienced as a blow to self-esteem, a dismissing of your past contributions to the workplace. Similarly, retiring because of job stress can feel like personal failure. Even when a difficult workplace is left behind, residual trauma is a possibility that can lead to periods of anxiety and depression. Negative emotions such as these can have flow-on effects, putting strain on your spouse, family and friendships and exacerbating the situation further. Such setbacks may be partially ameliorated by factors like a generous redundancy payout (if you are lucky enough to receive one!), a supportive family and social group, interests and goals you wish to pursue outside of the workplace, good health and personal resilience.

If retirement feels premature or pressured, one strategy for coping is to seek other work, even if it is not at the status level or time fraction to which you have been accustomed. A bridging period of part-time or casual employment, if available, can aid the transition to retirement by allowing more time for planning and 'getting used to' the idea. It is also helpful to be able to talk through your disappointments and develop new life plans with someone who is detached and non-judgemental, such as a counsellor.

WHEN YOU'VE GOT ENOUGH MONEY

As we mention on many occasions throughout this book, it will be much more satisfying if you can retire with adequate savings and pension entitlements to meet your lifestyle requirements.

How much do you need? This is not an easy question to answer. But before you make a decision to retire based on finances, it is important to gain a sense of the income you will need to maintain a comfortable lifestyle. What exactly are your entitlements? Do you have a sense of your day-to-day expenses and how are they likely to change in retirement? How long do you expect to live? Do you have any debts or any major expenses coming up? Have you made plans for post-retirement travel, house renovations or other big spends? Would you be prepared financially if faced with a significant but unexpected expense, such as a health crisis? Other important questions to ask yourself include whether there are part-time or casual jobs available if you need to top up your savings, and whether your current investments are performing adequately. The general state of the economy can have a marked effect on retirement plans, as evidenced by the Global Financial Crisis of 2008 that saw many people delay their retirement to earn back some of the funds they had lost when the stock market fell.

A sensible plan is to seek advice from a financial counsellor or trusted economic advisor if you are not sure about your financial status. If you believe your finances are inadequate, consider the pros and cons of working another year or two, perhaps in a different job. Interestingly, it is not uncommon for people to work well beyond their need to economically support a comfortable retirement because they enjoy their job and feel healthy and motivated to continue longer. Everybody is different.

WHEN YOUR HEALTH TELLS YOU

It's not only poor health that can lead to a decision to retire. Sometimes it is good health. One thing people do as they enter their senior years is speculate on how much time they have left. In relation to the things you want to experience and achieve in life – your bucket list – this can be a mind-focussing exercise. Many are motivated to retire while still in good health, 'before it is too late'. Retirees we talked to gave advice like 'travel early in your retirement, while you still have your health' and 'don't wait too long to do the things you really want to do'.

Retiring because your physical or mental health is poor is, of course, far less satisfying, a conclusion backed up by ample research. While retirement allows greater opportunities to rest, relax and respond to treatment, the transition in itself can be stressful – as we have seen – with the potential to exacerbate negative mood, especially if you are socially isolated. Can you take some sick leave instead, ask to be assigned to lighter duties or work part-time? For some, these options may allow heath to be maintained or chronic illness symptoms stabilised. Retirement can be worked toward more gradually and social supports put in place to assist not only with health care but also with making the change from worker to retiree.

WHEN YOU'RE READY TO DISENGAGE FROM YOUR JOB

Being in a job you love can be a great buzz. People who are lucky enough to work at what they enjoy are more likely to delay retirement. Higher levels of education are associated with delayed retirement, perhaps because the well-educated are more likely to be in occupations that are interesting, fulfiling and associated with better working conditions. Those who live for their work, are 'workaholics' and/or cannot imagine life without the challenges of their occupation will tend to put off retirement and may find the transition a difficult one, a topic we discuss in more detail in Chapter 6.

WHEN THE STARS OF FAMILY LIFE ARE IN ALIGNMENT

Women are far more likely than men to cite family reasons for retiring. Studies indicate that married women tend to coordinate their retirement date with their partner's retirement intentions often so they can retire together.[8] Couples are more likely to time their retirements to coincide if they enjoy each other's company.[9] A significant proportion of retired women we surveyed said they retired for family reasons, including the desire to spend time with their partner, travel together and share activities. Some commented on how successful this had been; others were disappointed that their husbands 'did not want to get off the couch' or that their relationship was not standing up well to both being home all day. Sadly, the plans of some women had to be adapted or abandoned when their partners fell ill or died early in the retirement years.

Another key family reason for retirement is to care for grandchildren. A large-scale longitudinal study in the US showed that the arrival of a new grandchild increased the probability of a woman retiring by 8 per cent.[10] We have spoken to many grandmothers who either retired or moved to part-time work in order to assist with grandchildren and bond with them in their pre-school years.

In comparison to retiring to have fun with a loved spouse or enjoy your grandchildren's childhoods, retirement for some family reasons can be extremely stressful. Examples include the need to leave the workforce to take on full-time caring responsibilities for an elderly relative, a disabled spouse or grandchildren whose parents cannot cope.

Even if leaving the paid workforce to spend more time with family is for the happiest of reasons, there can be relationship stresses. Household roles and responsibilities may need renegotiating. Expect a period of adjustment. If family pressures to retire present difficult and challenging circumstances, adjustment will take longer and your coping resources will be stretched. It is important to consider all your options, seek the support of others and not become a martyr to your caring responsibilities, an issue discussed further in Chapter 5.

WHEN THERE ARE OTHER THINGS YOU WANT TO DO BESIDES WORK

You've always wanted to study archaeology, set up a local catering business, learn Italian, write your family history, play more golf, go deep sea fishing or travel to far-flung places. Retirement can be your time. As one of our study participants said, 'Full-time work became too demanding with all my other commitments and hobbies!' One of the most satisfying reasons to retire is to take up interests and activities that you are passionate about. Even when goals don't quite come to fruition – like trying to learn the piano at age 65 (possible but very difficult) – you can have fun trying.

So, there is no ideal age to retire that will suit everyone. It's best though if you can choose your own time, when you are ready to leave behind or modify your workplace identity and seek other challenges. It's best if you are not pressured to leave by work, family or health concerns, and when your finances and social networks allow you to maintain a comfortable, connected lifestyle and indulge in interests and activities you enjoy. Of course, life does not always follow an idealised course. Luckily, we humans are an adaptable species. It is also worth noting that retirement decisions need not be irreversible for everybody. Bridge employment, casual work or even new careers are desirable and achievable options for many retirees.

3

FINANCIAL SECURITY OR FINANCIAL STRESS?

Retirement is expensive; the bills come in but not the income.[1]

Financial security is perhaps the most important single issue for retirees. Whether retirees have adequate financial resources for their retirement is of critical concern not only to retirees themselves but also to the community at large, given the cost implications of financial poverty among a relatively large (and increasing) sector of the population.

Retirement can become a time of poverty with a significant number of people finding themselves in financial and psychological stress as their retirement years add up. Indeed, many retirees enter this period of their life without the necessary savings or entitlements to support them as they age. Furthermore, men are financially better off than women post-retirement. We shall see that financial security or lack of it is perhaps the most dramatic example of gender differences among retirees.

Traditionally retirement financial resources have derived from three 'pillars': personal superannuation contributions by employers and employees while working, government pensions and savings. Superannuation is designed to ensure funds are available for a comfortable retirement, but the balance available on retirement suggests this is unlikely, especially for women whose funds, on average, are half those of men. Low wealth, little or no retirement savings and longer life expectancy result in many having to rely on government pensions as their main or only source of retirement income. And even in wealthy Western countries pensions are often barely adequate to sustain even a modest post-retirement lifestyle.

Worryingly, in Australia about one-third of men and women retire without any superannuation, totally dependent on pensions and savings for retirement living. In other countries employer-based contributions are equally low and in some, non-existent. Another potential problem, particularly for women, who tend to retire earlier than men, is that early retirement is likely to lead to them spending their financial resources and thus not only having less accumulated superannuation but also less wealth.

In 2016 the Statistic Brain Research Institute in the US provided useful data about savings for retirement in that country. The average savings of a 50-year-old was under $50,000 and the average net worth of a 55–64-year-old was even less. Not surprisingly, Statistics Brain estimates that only 4 per cent of those who start working at the age of 25 will have adequate capital stowed away for retirement at age 65.[2] For those who have saved carefully for their retirement, other factors may reduce their nest egg. Taxation results in loss of savings income; savings are not protected from inflation unless wisely invested (which requires effort and knowledge); savings may have been sufficient when people did not live as long as they do now, but would need to be much higher to provide an income stream for 20–30 years as is now often required.

Many Americans are not prepared for retirement says a recent report[3] that found nearly half of families have no retirement account savings at all. According to the Economic Policy Institute, the *mean* retirement savings of all families is just under $100,000. But many families have zero savings and 'super-savers' can increase the mean or average; a better estimate is the median savings, or those at the 50th percentile. The *median* savings for all families in the US is just $5,000.

It's just as bad for retirees in the UK where a 2017 report[4] showed one in seven people due to retire in 2017 admit to having no workplace or personal retirement savings and 11 per cent of those retiring in 2017 expect to be totally or somewhat reliant on the state pension in old age. A worker retiring and relying solely on the new flat-rate State Pension would have an income falling short of estimates of the minimum standards by a substantial amount. Not surprisingly financial stress in retirement was reported by more than one in three who said they were struggling to make ends meet.

THE GENDER GAP

I would never have handed over all my wages to my husband, nor co-signed loans for his business, or become guarantor for anyone. I regret being financially disabled all my married life of 47 years. Life has taken a definite downturn since I retired – I live from pension to pension.

The gender gap in wages is a key driver in women's poorer resources on retirement. Most retirement income systems do not take account of the different work patterns of women and men and structurally favour those who work full time without breaks for their entire work life. If you do not fit this pattern, you are significantly handicapped when saving for your retirement.

There are a number of interrelated work, family and societal factors that influence the pay gap. Women typically occupy lower paid roles in the workforce and lower paid occupations than men; they are more likely than men to work part-time or casually; and they are more likely to take breaks in their employment for childrearing or to provide unpaid care for others. Largely because of these responsibilities women have a more precarious attachment to the workforce, often working in casual jobs. Additionally, discrimination, both direct and indirect, still exists with women only recently being accepted in roles that were previously men's exclusive domain, such as mechanics, pilots, engineers and truck drivers.

A commonly cited example of this phenomenon is the gender difference in Chairs and/or Chief Executive Officers of major public companies. One might suggest that women are seriously disadvantaged by this, given the importance of these roles for company equity policies, including an understanding of women's particular work patterns, and their potential influence of these individuals on government policy.

In all countries where senior executives salaries are examined, women are hardly represented. In the US, the Standard & Poor's 500 index (S&P 500) is an index of 500 stocks seen as a leading indicator of equities. Women currently hold only 29 (5.8 per cent) CEO positions in these companies. In Australia in 2012, women remained under-represented in the most senior corporate positions within the top 200 companies listed on the Australian stock exchange. Six boards (3 per cent) had a woman as Chair and seven (different) companies had a female Chief Executive Officer (3.5 per cent). (In an amusing but telling anecdote, among these 200 companies, men named Peter or John were three times more likely than a woman to be a CEO or company). Similar data are available for the European Union, although Brexit may result in changes for those in the UK. There are only eight countries – France, Latvia, Finland, Sweden, UK, Denmark, Italy and Germany – in which women account for at least a quarter of board members.[5]

Looking more broadly at the gender differential in pay, a recent OECD report showed in 2014 the difference between women's and men's median wage varied dramatically from 3.3 per cent in Belgium to 36.7 per cent in South Korea. Most Western countries including the UK, US, Australia and Germany had a gap of around 17–19 per cent. In no country did women earn more than men. In the US, the average woman's annual salary has been cited as about four-fifths that of the average man's.[6]

The situation is worse if we turn to the lifetime accumulation of assets (the gender wealth gap). Not unexpectedly women fare badly relative to men. Women not only have less total wealth than men, they also have less diverse assets and are more likely than men to have their assets in a family home; in fact, the family home has become the key form of wealth for many women. Another factor contributing to the gender wealth gap is women's earlier retirement from the workforce compared to men. Early retirement is likely to lead to drawing down of financial resources, while retiring later has clear economic benefits, including earned wages, and possibly employer-provided health insurance and retirement plan contributions. These financial benefits accrue rapidly; for example, we know that working two more years has a significant impact on the preservation of retirement wealth for American workers.

FINANCIAL PLANNING

I am a grasshopper. I lived from pay to pay. I did not save or plan.

I applied the ideals about being financially savvy. I was most of my life, because I attended a very good seminar when I was very young, so I got my financial savviness from that.

Would it surprise you to know that our first quote is from a woman and the second from a man? Without wishing to reinforce stereotypes, these quotes encapsulate the differences between many women and men in their financial planning for retirement. Numerous studies find that women's planning for retirement has not matched their concerns about the need for financial security. In several studies nearly double the number of men compared with women claimed they were mostly responsible for financial and retirement planning in their households.

Interestingly, a recent US nationwide study showed that most retirees, and more women than men, wanted help from a professional in managing their investments, especially for specific aspects of retirement planning such as budgeting.[7] There was also considerable demand for help with their overall financial 'health'. Why the lack of planning and the need for outside help?

FINANCIAL LITERACY

The most common measure of financial literacy, and one that is used in most if not all research on this topic, consists of three questions about interest, inflation and risk diversification.[8] Although a limited measure, the questions do cover concepts most relevant to savings and investment decisions.

1 **Interest Rate Question**: Suppose you had $100 in a savings account and the interest rate was 2% per year. After 5 years, how much do you think you would have in the account if you left the money to grow? More than $102; Exactly $102; Less than $102; Do not know; Refuse to answer.

2 **Inflation Question**: Imagine that the interest rate on your savings account was 1% per year and inflation was 2% per year. After 1 year, how much would you be able to buy with the money in this account? More than today; Exactly the same; Less than today; Do not know; Refuse to answer.

3 **Risk Diversification Question**: Please tell me whether this statement is true or false. 'Buying a single company's stock usually provides a safer return than a stock mutual fund'. True; False; Do not know; Refuse to answer

You might like to test your own level of financial literacy by answering these questions![9]

There is abundant evidence of the importance of financial literacy in achieving and maintaining financial security. Unfortunately, a key driver of many people's difficulties in trying to save is their relative lack of financial literacy limiting their capacity to invest wisely. Worldwide data suggest that levels of literacy are low across most countries and lower for women than men. Many studies have confirmed this gender difference, across a range of nations. A 2017 report by the Global Financial Literary Excellence Center (2017) covering many countries found, on average, only one-third of adults demonstrated 'adequate' financial literacy, with lower rates for women than men.[10]

A comprehensive literature review of financial literacy research[11] confirmed what they termed the 'severe' levels of financial illiteracy among women, especially among single women and widows.

Why is it important to be financially literate? There is considerable agreement that financial literacy has a positive impact on financial behaviour and financial status. Financially literate individuals do better at a range of financial behaviours, including budgeting, saving money and planning for retirement. The link between literacy and important financial decisions means that women are particularly disadvantaged when it comes to planning for retirement and accumulating retirement wealth.

FINANCIAL RISK

A second key driver in increasing retirement wealth is the extent to which people are willing to make financially risky decisions. Conservative decisions are those that involve taking few risks with your savings and investments, for example putting money into low-interest but safe bank accounts or only buying blue chip stocks and shares. Such cautious behaviour is likely to be relatively safe but often means that the growth of your retirement nest egg will not keep up with inflation. If your retirement savings increase by 2 per cent per year, but the cost of food and housing goes up by 5 per cent over the same period you will be worse off financially. On the other hand, high-risk investment strategies are ones that can make or break you. These are strategies to be used sparingly unless you have deep pockets and/or have done your research thoroughly.

Moderate financial risk taking is advised by financial experts as the most effective investment strategy in the longer term. This generally involves diversifying assets, so that risk is spread over a range of different options, at a range of different risk levels – not putting all your eggs in the one basket. One hopes these strategies will allow investments to keep up with inflation while remaining relatively safe.

Financial risk aversion refers to over-reliance on low-risk investment strategies. While sensible in the short term, across the longer term of saving for retirement, being financially risk-averse will usually result in lower asset levels for the retiree. Financial risk has been the subject of many past research studies with the extremely robust result that women are more risk-averse than men. Coupled with poor financial literacy, risk-averse attitudes to financial investment over their work life may leave women at a disadvantage compared to men, and often without the ability or willingness to make the best possible financial decisions before or during retirement. Nothing has changed since these earlier studies in terms of male-female differences, although current research tends to be more interested in the reasons for this rather than simply the existence of difference.

Why are women more risk-averse than men? One explanation relates to gender inequalities in wealth and the different roles that impact on these inequalities, including gender discrimination in labour and credit markets, investment advice and information on investment decision-making. If your income is low, there is a lot to be lost by taking financial risks and, on balance, it may seem as though there is little to be gained.

Taking a 'tongue in cheek' approach but one based on the evidence, a senior economist followed the typical advice given to women for increasing their post-retirement financial security with his own commentary.[12]

1 Don't go into the caring professions. Don't. You will never, ever, match men's super if you 'choose' low paid work.
2 Don't take time out of the labour market to care for children. If you understand the genius of compounding interest, you'll know that the more you put away when you're young, the more you'll have when you're old. So if you 'choose' to take five or ten years out of the workforce to care for kids, don't come and complain later when your super balance is a little low.
3 Don't take time out of the workforce when you're older to care for your parents, or your partner's parents. Don't do that.
4 And this is the summary one: be a man.

Perhaps the last word should be left to one of our anonymous survey respondents. Asked what they would do differently, many women wrote at length and in negative terms about financial issues.

> I would try not to have breaks from paid employment, so that I would have been able to contribute more to superannuation. I would have been able to contribute longer to super (super did not exist when I first started working). I would have found out more about financial investment prior to retirement. I would have tried to have funds available to start investing in the property market sooner (for most of my early working life I lived pay to pay as I was a single mother with one wage).

Given that financial planning has clear benefits for a comfortable retirement the task for policy makers is to encourage and support individuals to plan wisely well in advance of leaving the paid workforce.

A KEY CONSEQUENCE OF FINANCIAL STRESS

> I expect to be poor; I may become functionally homeless.

Financial stress can have many negative consequences for retirees, requiring or leading to significant changes in lifestyle. Of these, the need to leave one's home is a major outcome. At least one study has shown late mid-life workers and retirees expect to remain at home as they age, but for retirees living in circumstances of financial stress, this is often not an option. It's costly to maintain a family home and this can be beyond the limited financial resources of some retirees. While the need to seek other housing may be due to a number of factors other than financial stress (such as poor health, serious chronic illness or death of a partner), loss of income on retirement is a major reason for seeking lower-cost accommodation. The need for this is especially acute for single female retirees who do not (and did not) have the earnings of a partner to help with finances. As one woman said: 'I was paying about 70 per cent of my income, which was a pension, on rent'. Even those with a small nest egg find they have to access this if they are on a pension in order to survive in an increasingly expensive private rental market.

> I previously rent[ed] on my own but due to the rent going up I couldn't keep up with it, and have had to move in with my friend who has Parkinson's [disease] and is not a stimulating or interesting person to be around. I've been forced to do this in order to save some money, but I can assure you that it is certainly not from choice.

For retirees who are renters, there is a potential loss of security of tenure as well as difficulties in finding suitable accommodation at an affordable cost, as the above quote indicates.

What options do retirees have if they cannot remain in their pre-retirement home? Retirement villages are a common choice, although there have been serious concerns raised about the financial costs of these. Other options available include downsizing to a smaller alternative or to move to a cheaper location. Although either may result in a better financial situation they can also involve less positive outcomes such as losing a cohort of neighbourhood friends and having to develop a new social network. Moving in with children (and grandchildren) is another solution to financial problems, but this can be fraught with disagreement. Multigenerational living can save money but disputes around money are common if sharing of expenses is perceived to be unreasonable. Retirees may find it hard to give up their independence and chafe at having to abide by family rules. This problem can be overcome if there is a place where each person has some area which is private, like the 'granny flat' of old that allowed for separate living with the security of having family nearby and with significant cost savings. Whatever the option taken there are costs as well as benefits in leaving one's family home after retirement. And for some retirees with very little in the way of financial resources, homelessness may be the ultimate end result.

BEWARE THE SCAM: A FINANCIAL TRAP

An all-too-common financial problem for retirees and other older adults is their willingness to risk financial security for easy financial gain. While there's no way to know how many people are impacted by this financial abuse, estimates are that nearly one in four seniors have been scammed. Why is this happening, as we know that many, especially women, are risk-averse?

Most of us are familiar with the Nigerian scam, designed to relieve us of money in order to receive, at some later point, a substantial financial reward. Such scams or dishonest schemes abound, unfortunately, in which scammers attempt to cheat or swindle vulnerable individuals financially or in other ways. Financial scams targeting older people have become so prevalent that they are now considered 'the crime of the 21st century' according to one report. While there are no data separating out the scams experienced by retirees, it is clear that a growing pool of retirees are susceptible to exploitation.

Financial scams can be of many types. Perhaps the most common is when scammers use fake telemarketing calls to prey on older people, who as a group make twice as many purchases over the phone than the national average. Others use the Internet to operate their scams; still others prefer personal home visits. While using the Internet is a great skill at any age, many older people find this difficult, making them easier targets for automated Internet scams that are ubiquitous on the web and email programmes. Their unfamiliarity with the less visible aspects of browsing the web (firewalls and built-in virus protection, for example) makes seniors especially susceptible to scams. For example scammers will send email messages that appear to be from a legitimate company or institution, asking them to 'update' or 'verify' their personal information.

Another scheme designed to swindle is the investment scam. Investment scams involve convincing the individual to part with money on the promise of a questionable financial opportunity. Because many older people find themselves planning for retirement and managing their savings once they finish working, a number of investment schemes have been targeted at seniors looking to safeguard their cash for their later years. From pyramid schemes to complex financial products that many economists don't even understand, investment schemes have long been a successful way to take advantage of older people.

Door-to-door and home maintenance scams are our last example of financial exploitation. While many legitimate businesses sell things door-to-door, scammers also use this approach. These types of scams generally involve promoting goods and services that are of poor quality, or not delivered at all. Unscrupulous contractors convince victims they are in dire need of various home repairs. Then they overcharge them or take money before the projects are completed and then disappear.

IF YOU SUSPECT YOU'VE BEEN THE VICTIM OF A SCAM . . .

Tell someone you trust; don't be afraid or embarrassed. Others have had similar experiences, and there are people and organisations that can help. If you do nothing, you may be exposed to another scam and, at the least, you give scammers the opportunity to prey on others. Keep handy the phone numbers and resources you can turn to, including the local police and your bank. The best protection against scams is to know how scammers operate. Don't be pressured into making a decision; be suspicious of requests for money even if they seem official; verify the identity of the contact, e.g., by calling the relevant organisation directly; ignore phone calls or emails offering financial advice or opportunities; be suspicious of unexpected emails or letters advising you how to claim an inheritance or competition prize; and, importantly, be aware of and understand your consumer rights.

ELDER FINANCIAL ABUSE

Sometime thought of as a scam, elder financial abuse is not carried out by strangers, as are scams, but by someone known and trusted by the older person, usually a family member. Although only one aspect of elder abuse, financial abuse is by far the most common and is an increasing phenomenon in Western nations, as both lifespan and the cost of housing increase. Some have called this phenomenon 'inheritance impatience'. Adult children can become frustrated at being unable to afford housing or other aspects of lifestyle while perceiving their parents to be 'sitting on resources' such as the family home, 'wasting' their inheritance on retirement leisure activities, distributing their finances unequally among their children or even threatening to leave their money to charity. More likely to be the victims of elder financial abuse are seniors who live alone, are socially isolated, have cognitive deficits and/or who rely on a family member for care. In worst-case scenarios, the elderly person can be inveigled or tricked into selling their family home, changing their will or limiting their quality of life in ways that are unnecessary, given their resources. There is a profound psychological impact as a result of this form of abuse. Understandably, the victims are likely to feel devastated when members of their family who they thought they could trust disappoint them. There is often a feeling of isolation because they can't rely on the people who surround them.

There are organisations, such as Seniors Right in Australia and Action on Elder Abuse in the UK, available to provide advice and support to victims of elder abuse. Discussing family finances with your adult children early in your retirement years, making a legal will, appointing a legal power of attorney (and choosing that person wisely) and acting early in cases where you (or other members of your family) suspect financial abuse are all strategies that may lessen the financial, emotional and psychological impact of this traumatic experience.

FINANCIAL SECURITY OR FINANCIAL STRESS?

What are the answers to the questions we posed at the beginning of this chapter? Not all retirees face financial stress and, potentially, poverty after they retire. Some have accumulated sufficient savings in one form or another to last them what might be many years of retirement. But many others find themselves wondering how they will survive these years. Some may have a small nest egg to help; others may be wholly reliant on a (usually inadequate) pension. We have seen that women, especially single women, are especially vulnerable, given their lower incomes over their working lives compared to men and their unstable careers due to factors like childrearing or caring for family members.

Clearly we need to create policies that will change the gender pay gap and ensure retirement is not a stage of life during which financial stress governs the lives of many retirees. Looking at OECD data for pension policies across many countries, it's evident that one size does not fit all and that policies must be framed around each country's demographics and financial resources. Key concerns identified include increasing the retirement age, ensuring financial sustainability of pension systems and providing a safety net for low-income earners. As OECD Director General Angel Gurría concludes about pension policy:

> Further reforms are needed that are both fiscally and socially responsible. We cannot risk a resurgence of old age poverty in the future. This risk is heightened by growing earnings inequality in many countries, which will feed through into greater inequality in retirement.[13]

4

RETIREMENT, HEALTH AND WELLBEING
IS RETIREMENT GOOD FOR YOUR HEALTH?

You've worked hard for many years and now you are retired. All those stressors – gone! All that structure to your day – gone! All the effort of trying to fit too many tasks into one day – gone! How will this change affect your health and life expectancy?

It's complicated. When moving from work to non-work, everything about your daily schedule changes. You may be more relaxed, and your life may slow down. Loss of work-related stress may be a great relief and good for your health, but losing the daily structure and your work relationships can also be stressful and harmful to your health. In fact, retirement is ranked 10th on the list of life's most stressful events. Predicting how retirement affects health is extremely difficult because retirement goes hand in hand with ageing, and retirees are, for the most part, older than those still working. Thus what might seem to be a consequence of retirement can be simply part of the ageing process. The relationship between retirement and health is an important one to consider given the shifting trends in labour force attachment, ageing of the population and growth in the cost of health care.

We noted earlier the dramatic increase in life expectancy through the 20th century and, correspondingly, longer periods spent in retirement. The remarkable improvements in life expectancy over the past century were part of a shift in the leading causes of disease and death. There is now considerable literature naming advances in medicine as one factor responsible for increased life expectancy, including the change in types of illness or disease from communicable diseases to chronic, non-communicable diseases and disability.[1]

Even in low-income countries, the majority of older people die from chronic diseases such as cardiac disease, cancer and diabetes rather than infectious diseases. One major health consequence of a longer lifespan is the increase in prevalence of dementia. This places considerable demands on the health care system, on long-term care, and on wellbeing of family members, especially the primary carer. The World Health Organisation notes that the risk of dementia rises sharply with age with an estimated 25–30 per cent of people ages 85 years or older showing some evidence of dementia.

What do we know about health and retirement? Is finally quitting the workplace good for you or not? Research indicates that mental health issues occur relatively infrequently post-retirement but physical health problems are relatively common, although often associated with ageing rather than retirement *per se*. So let's begin with a consideration of physical health. Is retirement associated with physical health improvements?

THE 'NO' CASE

A recent prospective study by the highly regarded Harvard School of Public Health investigated the association between transition to retirement and risk of stroke and heart attack. They followed participants aged 50 and over who were in the paid workforce and free of major cardiovascular disease up to 10 years until they retired. After adjusting for a wide range of factors (age, sex, socio-economic status, behaviour and co-morbidities), the researchers found that retirees were 40 per cent more likely to have had a heart attack or stroke than those who were still working at the same age. There were no differences between men and women in these outcomes.

Outcomes of a large UK study showed almost twice the number of retired individuals compared to those still employed at the same age suffered chronic conditions such as diabetes, stroke or cancer. Women retirees had a higher risk than the overall sample of being diagnosed with cancer and a lower risk of developing cardiovascular diseases. Male retirees were more at risk than the overall sample for heart attack, stroke and psychiatric problems. However, the author notes that poorer health outcomes among retirees compared to those still working cannot be regarded solely as the result of retirement, even after adjusting for age. Poor health is often one of the reasons people retire, rather than a result of the process of retirement. Nevertheless, as we discuss later in the chapter, there may be some factors associated with retirement that lead to worsening health, for example an increase in social isolation or adoption of bad health habits.

THE 'YES' CASE

Not all research shows detrimental effects of retirement. Consistent with a number of studies, one recent study, across 12 Western European countries, using rigorous methods, showed that retirement can lead to improvements in self-reported health, across educational levels and for men and women alike.[2] Further, in the US Normative Aging Study of men, although men's physical health declined over three to four years, there were no differences between those who were still working and those who had retired.

Equally positive are the findings from recent German research.[3] The study author concluded that retiring from work is good for your health, chiefly due to the benefits of more exercise, less stress and greater sleep enjoyed by people who stop working. In retirement, people are more likely to rate their health as satisfactory. Mental health improves, even after allowing for age-related medical problems and for those retired early due to ill health. The author estimated that the number of doctor visits reduced by 25 per cent for retirees compared to non-retirees of the same age, an important finding for the economics of the German health system. It would be interesting to see this research replicated in other countries.

Nevertheless, as both the proportion of older people in communities and the length of life increase throughout the world, key questions arise. Will population ageing be accompanied by a longer period of good health, a sustained sense of wellbeing, and extended periods of social engagement and productivity? Or will it be associated with more illness, disability and dependency? These questions are important not only in terms of providing best practice preparation for retirement and subsequent health care but also because of policy moves in some countries to raise the age at which state pensions become available, with a view to inducing postponed retirement.

WHAT INFLUENCES RETIREMENT HEALTH?

I did not expect retirement to be this good. I feel that I am fortunate to be in good health, and able to enjoy life as it is.

I expected my health to be better, and to be more mobile than I am. This is restricting me in many ways. . . . I can no longer join some friends for brisk walks, hikes with backpacks etc.

What is behind these two contrasting experiences of health in retirement? As we saw earlier, there is equivocal evidence regarding the health consequences of retirement with some studies showing positive effects, others negative. Issues which may affect health outcomes in retirement include social connectedness/support, participation in physical exercise, post-retirement lifestyle (e.g., changes in smoking or alcohol use), being married, gender, post-retirement activities, whether retirement was voluntary and whether retirement was earlier than the normative age.

One thought-provoking link with poor health is the experience of loneliness and social isolation. While not specifically a problem of retirees, retirement may trigger increased loneliness and decreased social connections. There is strong evidence that social isolation and loneliness heighten the risk for premature mortality and that this risk exceeds that of many key ill-health indicators. Researchers have shown that loneliness can be a bigger killer than obesity and should be considered a major public health issue. A review of 218 studies into the health effects of social isolation and loneliness[4] found that lonely people have a 50 per cent higher chance of premature death, while obesity increases the chance of early death by 30 per cent. The team found that the risk of early death associated with loneliness, social isolation and living alone was equal to or greater than the premature death risk associated not only with obesity but with other major health conditions.

Another factor relates to lifestyle changes post-retirement. Some people improve their nutrition and exercise regimes; others do not. For example, in a large study of Australian women in 2016,[5] retirement status had positive effects on women's self-reported health, physical and mental health outcomes. These positive effects were linked to increased physical activity post-retirement and reduced smoking. On the other hand a Finnish study demonstrated that while women tended to improve their dietary habits when they retired, this was not the case for retired men.[6]

A long-term study of British civil servants reinforces the need for care in concluding that retirement affects health, either positively or negatively. On-time retirement and voluntary early retirement were both related to better physical functioning and mental health when retirees were compared to those who remained in the workforce. The authors suggested that there might be a causal relationship between voluntary retirement and positive health outcomes. However we need here to consider the possibility of including selection bias. For example, those who choose earlier retirement may do so either because their health is compromised or because they are healthy and want to enjoy retirement activities while still fit enough to do so. Certainly, there is evidence from our study of Australian women that a significant minority retire voluntarily, but many do so for health reasons (15 per cent), because of work stress (19 per cent) or the ill health of family members (11 per cent). We need to tease out what is meant by 'voluntary' retirement.

A number of studies have used careful methodologies, including sophisticated sampling methods, and analyses that adjust for selection bias (e.g., pre-retirement work and health history, timing of retirement) to overcome these difficulties. In the analysis of data from seven waves of the US Health and Retirement Study[7] these biases accounted for most of the observed differences in health between retirees and non-retirees over time. The authors concluded the adverse health effects are mitigated if the individual is married and has social support, continues to engage in physical activity post-retirement or continues to work part-time upon retirement. There was also some evidence that the adverse health effects are larger in the event of involuntary retirement, a finding consistent with other studies.

Is early retirement a healthy idea? Some studies have similarly shown that early retirement has negative consequences for post-retirement physical and emotional health and cognitive functioning, although, in respect of the last, there is recent evidence that work that requires higher mental demands is protective against cognitive decline in retirement independent of education level and socio-economic status. At least one study has shown that people who retired at age 55 had almost twice the risk of death compared to people who retired at age 60. The link between early retirement and early death was greater for men than women; men who retired at 55 had an 80 per cent greater increase risk than women who retired at 55.

In the relatively narrow age range of older women in our study (mostly in their 60s), age was not related to health *per se*, but it was related to changes in health. Women's health was deteriorating as they aged, as shown by worsening health among those who had been retired longer. But there are large individual differences in when this process begins. For example, those whose health got better on retirement were more likely to have retired younger than those whose health stayed the same, but then so were those whose health got worse post-retirement. This fits with the idea that women who choose earlier retirement may do so either because their health is compromised or because they are healthy and want to enjoy retirement activities while still fit enough to do so.

There are many challenges with estimating the impact of retirement on health apart from the confounding of retirement with ageing as we have seen. The difficulty in establishing clear links between physical health and retirement suggests it may prove more productive to examine psychological health. The most commonly researched marker of mental health in retirement is depression while another approach is to determine how individuals' adjust to retirement and how satisfied they are with this life transition.

PSYCHOLOGICAL WELLBEING

I thought that I was ready to retire mentally – but found that it actually took me three years to adjust – I grieved for my job and that process took that long. There was no help or recognition about the grieving process. I had to work through that myself, and it was only after I came out the other end that I realized what had happened to me.

Psychological wellbeing refers to the extent to which an individual experiences life in a positive way and functions well psychologically and is often described in studies of retirees as 'adjustment', although few researchers have actually measured pre- and post-retirement psychological adjustment specifically. Most rely on life satisfaction or satisfaction with retirement as a surrogate for this.

The majority of retirees report little or no change in psychological wellbeing post-retirement. Our study of retired women measured two adjustment-like measures, self-esteem and stress levels. When asked if their self-esteem was better, the same or worse than before they retired, most reported 'same' while one-quarter reported higher self-esteem post-retirement. Higher levels of self-esteem were associated with significantly better health post-retirement, as well as greater satisfaction with their health. Asked about stress, three-quarters reported being less stressed and only 7 per cent were more stressed after they retired.

An extensive review of the literature[8] noted that research into the association between life satisfaction and retirement has produced inconsistent findings and is partly dependent on pre-retirement levels of life satisfaction.

What of depression in retirement? Depression is an important health problem in many countries. It reduces productivity at work and is the fastest increasing reason for early retirement. There is convincing evidence that depression is associated with increased risk of early retirement, and depressed individuals retire at a significantly younger age than those without depression. Post-retirement depression has also been documented but less convincingly. For example, while an Institute of Economic Affairs report[9] showed being retired increased risk of clinical depression by 40 per cent, not all studies have demonstrated such a strong effect and some, none at all. There is clearly more research needed here to tease out the effects of pre-retirement psychological health, retirement, social isolation, ageing and lifestyle factors on depression.

WHAT PREDICTS PSYCHOLOGICAL ADJUSTMENT AFTER RETIREMENT?

Psychological wellbeing and adjustment are greatly dependent on all the resources that individuals bring to the retirement transition. These resources can be personal, material or social and are drawn on to help individuals manage stressful or difficult situations.[10] While many (most?) retirees have little or no difficulty in negotiating retirement, some appear not to have the resources to refashion their lives. For example, in our study, the word 'boring' recurred frequently as women complained about the 'emptiness' of their retirement lives.

> It can be tedious, boring and even though I am a loner, more solitary than I would sometimes like. I don't fit much of the community programs and even some of the other activities that are around.

Lower levels of wellbeing are likely to result from external factors such as a partner's poor health or because of demanding family caring responsibilities, as these restrict opportunities to take up new roles in retirement. The gendered expectations of caring mean that women are more likely to regard caring for a partner as an obligation and spend more time doing so than men, a state of affairs that has been linked to increased stress.

Another concern for retirees who have spent many years in the workforce, with tasks clearly prescribed, is the lack of structure to their day.

> It's hard to build structure into a life that suddenly becomes freefalling.

Additionally, for those whose sense of self is tied to their work identity, retirement can be a daunting prospect. The lack of challenges and excitement that daily work brought to their lives is reflected in loss of self-esteem and sense of contributing to society.

> I absolutely hate it. I find it financially challenging, lonely and boring. I feel as though I am brain dead, and I am being left further and further behind in learning new technologies and discovering new interests. . . . I find I am sinking into apathy and the less I do the less I want to do.

While these issues affect some but by no means the majority of retirees, the loss of financial resources is a major concern for many, especially women, as we have seen in Chapter 3. Inadequate finances can affect many aspects of life satisfaction, for example through limiting access to secure housing and adequate health care, and reducing opportunities to engage in new roles and activities because of their cost.

Since 2010, a number of reviews addressing the determinants of adjustment to life during retirement have been published, reflecting the growing interest in this field. A recent thorough review of predictors of adjustment to retirement[11] identified four groups of predictors. The most commonly reported predictors included physical health, finances, psychological health and personality-related attributes, leisure, voluntary retirement and social integration. There was a group of 'non' or 'negative' predictors of retirement adjustment that included age, sex, household composition, timing of retirement and ethnicity. In all these cases, the majority of studies found no effect of the variable in question on retirement adjustment or, at best, results were inconsistent.

This carefully conducted and substantial systematic review of the literature on predictors of retirement adjustment is important but it may leave the reader confused about contributions of specific individual factors. For example, in half the studies reviewed, participants who had been retired longer presented better quality of life, wellbeing and satisfaction with retirement and with life. Time since retirement had no effect in six studies, and only two studies indicated time was a risk factor for retirement.

Actively planning for retirement and retirement at a time of their own choosing are both positively related to retirees' psychological wellbeing. People who retire earlier than planned are more likely to experience decreased psychological wellbeing entering retirement.

The consequences of poor psychological wellbeing can be associated with retirees engaging in maladaptive behaviours. These behaviours can further compromise physical as well psychological wellbeing with implications for retirees' ability to plan and manage their retirement. As we have seen, some retirees miss the structure, the challenges and the companionship of their working lives, and some find replacement activities that are problematic for their physical and mental health. Two of the most common behaviours are substance abuse (both alcohol and drugs) and problem gambling.

SUBSTANCE ABUSE

Nearly a decade ago over one-quarter of women and half the men drank beyond the recommended guidelines for their age. Interestingly, other US data show rates of alcohol abuse and dependence increased almost 10-fold over a decade in women ages 65 and older. In contrast, among men ages 65 and older there was been four-fold increase.[12] To the extent that retirement is often framed by older adults as a major life event and by some a significant stressor, it may act as a risk factor for alcohol misuse. On the other hand, one could speculate that retirees have more leisure time to drink, among other activities, so alcohol use starts as positive enjoyment – providing a sense of freedom and lessening of responsibility. In fact, the link between retirement and alcohol misuse is not straightforward. Bamburger concludes two areas of consensus seem to be emerging. First, a variety of individual attributes and situational factors influence this link probably by influencing the way in which retirement is framed. If retirement is framed as 'loss', alcohol misuse may be initiated or made worse, while a frame of 'relief' may result in a decline in misuse. Second, the consensus is that retirement does not directly affect drinking behaviour, but the context of retirement (why the decision to retire was made and the experiences before and after retirement) can trigger new or increased alcohol-use disorders among older adults.

DRUG ABUSE

Drug abuse among retirees and older people has focused largely on prescription drug use, by far the most common category of drug abuse among this group. Abuse of prescription drugs among older adults does not typically involve the use of these substances to 'get high' and the users do not usually obtain them illegally. Instead, unsafe combinations or amounts of medications may be obtained by seeking prescriptions from multiple doctors, by obtaining medications from family members or peers, or by stockpiling medications over time.

It is important to note, however, that substance abuse issues among the elderly represent a growing public health concern. According to 2017 data from the US Office of Alcoholism and Substance Use Services, 17 per cent of people over 65 in the US have abused prescription drugs. Clearly the link between retirement and drug abuse and the reasons for this need to be a greater focus of attention by researchers.

GAMBLING

Is excessive gambling a problem for retirees? Certainly the growth of casinos and slot machines catering to seniors suggests there is a problem. To cater to this population some casinos even supply wheelchairs and oxygen tanks! In fact, gambling, like alcohol consumption, exists along a continuum of involvement from not gambling at all, to social gambling, to problem gambling. Although more men than women gamble, women's progression to problematic gambling appears to be quicker than men's, with women likely to face financial difficulties sooner than men as they do not have the financial buffer that men have.

There is now considerable evidence of gender differences in gambling choices.[13] Men tend to gamble on games of 'skill' – card games such as poker, racing and other sports – and are characterised as 'action' gamblers. Women, however, are likely to be 'escape' gamblers, preferring activities such as bingo, lotteries or slot machines, and often gambling to reduce boredom, escape responsibility or relieve loneliness rather than for financial gain, pleasure or excitement. It seems that in the past two decades gambling has increasingly become a mainstream pastime for women, largely because of the expansion of electronic gaming machines. Suggested motivations for gambling include social isolation, the need to escape form everyday stress and psychological co-morbidity. In the case of the last, depression and anxiety disorders are key factors that coexist with problem gambling.

The literature we have reviewed indicates some consistent health and wellbeing consequences of retirement, but there are many factors whose impact is uncertain or contradictory. As we have seen, the challenge is to take into account the myriad of contextual factors associated with the transition to retirement and the experience of this life stage.

MAINTAINING GOOD HEALTH IN RETIREMENT

Physical activity, a balanced diet and sustaining a healthy weight are key factors in maintaining and enhancing good health together with moderation in alcohol intake and being a non-smoker. Retirement provides the opportunity to engage in physical activity that may have been limited by the demands of full-time work, and the positive link between retirement health and physical activity has been well documented, as already discussed.

It is feasible to expect changes in weight to be associated with retirement. On one hand, healthier habits in retirement such as increased physical activity and better diet are likely to lead to weight loss. On the other hand, weight gain may result from the body changes as one ages, from being less physically active, from having less structured meal times or from using food as a means of dealing with post-retirement losses such as work identity, social interactions at work or the sense of accomplishment resulting from working.

Where gender differences in weight change after retirement have been studied, the results are inconsistent. A prospective study of a large and stable French cohort included yearly and long-term measurements that enabled researchers to obtain accurate estimates of physical activity and changes in weight during the actual retirement transition. One analysis[14] showed that physical activity increased by 36 per cent among men and 61 per cent among women during the transition to retirement. Not surprisingly, weight gain was greater among physically inactive persons compared with those physically active. The observed increase in physical activity after retirement corroborates findings in many other studies, confirming the importance of post-retirement physical activity. In another study, there was no significant weight change among men, but women who had retired were more likely to gain weight than those who continued to work part-time, who were of normal weight upon retiring and those who retired from blue-collar occupations.

In contrast, results from another large-scale nationally representative cohort in the UK[15] showed, for most age groups, men were more likely than women to participate in regular physical activity (walking, swimming or playing sport) on a weekly basis. Interestingly, women reported lower subjective wellbeing than men. The authors speculate that this may be attributable to women's lower employment participation rates and lower income as well as their greater role as informal carers since these are all related to lower subjective wellbeing.

Of course, weight gain may not only be caused by less physical activity but by changing eating habits. One Finnish study found that healthy eating habits increased more among retired women than those continuously employed whereas among men healthy food habits were not associated with retirement. Possibly this gender difference can be explained by many retired women having more time and choosing to shop for and prepare healthy options; most men when they retire continue to eat the food that is provided for them.

As we age, the role of nutrition becomes even more important. We could locate no research examining the specific links between good nutrition and retirement, but it is reasonable to assume the importance of a good diet among retirees. There are many health benefits of a healthy diet and proper nutrition apart from weight loss. These include resistance to illness and disease, higher energy levels and increased mental sharpness. Good diet allows your body to function better. Eating a healthy mix of grains, fruits, vegetables, dairy and protein gives your body all of the nutrients it needs; you feel more awake, and you have more energy to spare. Eating fruits and vegetables is also believed to reduce your risk for certain cardiovascular diseases, stroke, type 2 diabetes and cancer.

A recent English survey showed a multi-year trend towards increasing levels of obesity with a quarter of all adults obese now compared to around 15 per cent in 1993, with the increase slightly quicker for men than women. The 'obesity epidemic' has profound public health effects because obesity increases the likelihood of diseases such as heart disease, diabetes and some kinds of cancer. More than three in every 10 people aged 55 to 64 and just heading into retirement were classed as obese. As the authors note dryly, after these ages obesity prevalence declines, possibly because the least healthy die off.

So, with a healthy diet, your body physically functions better and there are mental health benefits as well. A healthy diet can also boost mood and lower stress levels as well as protect you to some extent from disease.

PLAN FOR A HEALTHY RETIREMENT

How do we ensure good health in retirement? Sometimes retirement is a necessary outcome of poor health. Or the unexpected happens after we retire and we become ill in spite of all our efforts to remain healthy. Ageing itself is undeniably a health hazard. But as we have seen in this chapter, there are some fundamental lifestyle choices that will boost chances of a healthy retirement, both physically and mentally. It is important that pre-retirement plans include thinking about a healthy retirement lifestyle. Better still, start the process before retiring.

There is an abundance of self-help advice about how to maintain good health in retirement and it is remarkably consistent. Stay active and involved. Whether it's organised sports or activities, or taking long walks on your own, it's important to keep moving. Make sure you have regular medical checks, especially for age-related diseases, as well as dental and hearing checks given the importance of the last for communication.

Maintain a healthy diet – follow dietary recommendations about daily intake; exercise every day to build strength, flexibility, cardio-vascular health and balance.

If you can't or don't want to engage in sports or exercise activities there are other options that may fit your lifestyle better. Retirement can increase time invested in repairs, gardening, and other household activities. These require physical effort and can therefore be expected to enhance health by providing physical activity over and above the increase in sports and exercise.

Exercise your brain too; crosswords, puzzles and learning new things are some of the activities that help you to maintain your level of cognitive functioning. But take time to relax as well. Try meditation or yoga, maintain good sleep habits – 7 to 9 hours every night is optimal. Try to avoid daily naps. Importantly, maintain social connections. Try to banish loneliness. Your relationships with people can help you live longer. Nurture your friendships and family ties. If you are away from friends and family, think about making social connections in other ways such as through volunteering – it's a great way to meet people and get the health benefits of relationships too.

5

RENEGOTIATING SOCIAL RELATIONSHIPS

Social relationships are bound to undergo significant changes when you retire. There are new friends to be made, old friendship to be resumed, workplace collegiality to be maintained and family relationships to be renegotiated. Both opportunities and potential pitfalls accompany the different social spaces that retirees occupy, and there may be need for adjustment of expectations and proactivity in developing new friendships. In this chapter, we discuss these relationship patterns and how they change during retirement.

INTIMATE PARTNER RELATIONSHIPS

Many surveys and studies have indicated that marital relationships either improve or stay the same when couples retire. There is more time for partners to do things together, carry out long-held plans and dreams, perhaps make a sea change or tree change, travel or just relax. Intimacy can be enhanced, and couples may report that the depth of feeling for each other becomes even stronger as they share joys and sorrows of growing old together and watching their children and grandchildren mature. Research is clear that married retirees usually enjoy better psychological wellbeing than single or widowed retirees.[1]

It doesn't always work out this way. Partners spending so much more time together can discover they have far less in common than they realised when both were constantly busy with work and family. Expectations about activities in retirement, domestic responsibilities and extent of 'togetherness' can turn out to be very different and compromises difficult to achieve.

> I wish I had spent more time exploring my husband's vision of us in retirement. He saw it as us keeping each other company . . . and my being able to take back all the domestic chores. He doesn't like 'going out' and he doesn't like being left home alone . . . he sulks!

As well, in our studies, a number of women commented on the level of dependency shown by their spouses post-retirement.

> I find my husband needs me more than I need him. I can't go shopping without him coming or ringing to find out where I am and when I'll be home. This is hard to deal with as we were once both senior public servants and independent of each other.

Research suggests that retired men can find developing new social networks more difficult than do women, who tend to be more socially integrated, possibly because many have spent significant periods of their adult life outside of the paid workforce and so are more likely to have developed non-work friendship groups. Although there are many individual differences in sociability, it seems that retired men too often isolate themselves. For example, a large-scale time-use survey in Australia found that paradoxically, retired men spent *less* time with family and friends outside of the household than men still in the workforce. Retired women were the opposite, making use of their time in retirement to socialise with family and friends from outside their immediate household.[2]

Unfortunately, the intimate bond between some couples does not survive retirement, leading to late life divorce or separation, a phenomenon increasing along with our lifespans (and the expectation of many healthy years post-retirement). Divorce among the over 50s is becoming more common. Unsatisfied spouses may choose to end their marriage when their adult children leave home, deciding it is now or never to fulfil their dreams. Coping with partnership breakdown *and* the change of lifestyle accompanying retirement can put a major strain on personal resources, financially and emotionally.

> My wife and I were together for 35 years, and our financial affairs were so intertwined that it took a full year to disentangle them and sort out who got what. That was the easy part. It's the loneliness and heartbreak that is hard to bear.

A different family issue but one that is not uncommon during retirement is the death of a partner. As well as the sadness of bereavement, the death of a spouse means the loss of so many day-to-day interactions and shared activities, increasing the risk of loneliness and depression. Retirees can struggle to cope, especially in the early years of grieving. Plans need to be re-evaluated during this vulnerable time.

> I expected to be sharing retirement with my husband of 40 years. However, he was diagnosed with Stage 4 cancer in 2014 and died 25 months later.

A partner's poor health and need for care also restricts opportunities to take up new roles in retirement. These situations are likely to be associated with changes to the nature of the relationship between the ill person and their carer, as well as the possibility of compromised wellbeing for the carer. Gendered expectations surrounding nurturance mean that women are more likely to regard caring for a partner as an obligation, and spend more time doing so than men, a state of affairs that has been linked to increased stress. We discuss further aspects of the carer role in the next section.

FAMILY RELATIONSHIPS

Expectations that retirement will allow for more and enriched family time are not always realised. The busy lives of your adult children are unlikely to have altered just because you have retired. Your son or daughter may not choose to spend their day off work with you; they have their own lives to lead. Your retirement and the ageing process that accompanies it can also lead to family conflicts about where you live and how you choose to spend your money (as we discussed in Chapter 3).

Nevertheless, retirement does offer the opportunity to strengthen family relationships. Retirees, if they are able, can offer various forms of assistance to other family members, such as financial assistance, mentoring, help with chores and grandparenting duties. Research suggests this has reciprocal benefits. Retirees who regularly look after their grandchildren, or often help their children with practical tasks, experience more intergenerational support through their retirement transition compared with retirees who never provide these types of help.[3]

CARING FOR GRANDCHILDREN

For those who are lucky enough to have young grandchildren, assisting with babysitting and childcare can be a wonderful opportunity to create powerful bonds with the grandchildren as well as strengthen family relationships in general. In studies we have conducted, grandparents described many significant and life enhancing benefits arising from their role, including a new focus for their love and a source of joy and pleasure. Some retired specifically to spend more time with their grandchildren.

> Well I was working full-time when Lily was born and I worked a nine-day fortnight so I could have a day with her. And then I took retirement early, so the kids had a big influence on that I think. They sort of showed me there was more to life than working.

Now if I have the kids I can devote myself to them, I don't have to do a hundred other things at the same time.[4]

In Chapter 2 we discussed the concept of 'generativity'. This is the idea that a mature and healthy psychosocial development for one's middle and senior years involves contributing to the welfare of the next generation. Overall, the grandparents in our studies developed a stronger sense of generativity through their concern for, nurture and guidance of their children and grandchildren.[5] Other researchers have also noted the relationships between time spent looking after grandchildren, sense of generativity, overall satisfaction with life and even extended lifespan.[6]

Problems can occur when the expectations of retiree grandparents do not meet the expectations of parents. Sometimes the amount of childcare expected can be a cause for stress or conflict. One woman put it this way.

One daughter expects me to come whenever she calls for babysitting even though it disrupts my own plans. It is expected of me as I am the non-working grandmother.

Particularly stressful can be the situation in which grandparents must assume the full-time carer role for their grandchildren, usually because of some difficult or tragic family situation such as parental death, illness, drug addiction or criminality. In these cases, retirees can find themselves emotionally, physically and financially challenged. Many – perhaps most – make the best of it for the sake of their grandchildren, and still find love and joy in the strength of their relationships. Nevertheless, such situations are certainly a challenge to retirement plans for 'me time'!

CARING FOR ELDERLY RELATIVES

Elderly relatives or one's partner may also be in need of care. Because we are living longer, many retirees are likely to have frail or ill parents.

Women typically spend more than twice the amount in caring duties than men (and, perhaps unsurprisingly, brothers defer to their sisters when parental care is needed). Type of care is also differentiated by gender. Women are more likely than men to help with personal and daily domestic tasks while men more often undertake occasional tasks such as home repairs or installing equipment.[7] Studies show men and women who provide care for elderly family members report negative mental and physical health consequences, including a higher mortality rate. For retirees there is often significant stress in having to give up or delay substantially the plans they had made for how to spend their retirement. Indeed, the need to care for a partner or older relative can be an unanticipated outcome or a precipitator of retirement with the possible financial consequences that can accompany early retirement. Caring for the elderly can be challenging as these quotes illustrate.

> I am trapped – caring for a demanding and often aggressive elderly mother. I see no end in sight.

> All the planning in the world goes out the window when 'life' happens. My mother is 97. While she lives in supported accommodation, as her only relative in our town, I am her primary carer. All my plans to do a lot of walking travelling overseas just can't happen. That's life!!!!

Retirees who are full-time or even occasional carers for those who are elderly or ill are a vulnerable population. Even when the cared-for person is greatly cherished and easy to get on with, there are stresses to manage. Not the least of these is the eventual death of a loved partner, parent or relative, with the subsequent grief – and sometimes guilt – that this can bring. Depression, poor physical health, exhaustion, loneliness and social isolation are further risks of being a principal carer. Self-care is vital. Finding out what community resources are available, marshalling family and local support, taking time off through the use of respite care, maintaining friendships that are supportive and affirming, and keeping healthy are all important considerations for any carer, whether retired or not.

THE SPECIAL CASE OF SINGLES

> Being alone and single [in retirement] is stressful, lonely and embarrassing and socially limiting.

> Retirement brings with it (for me anyway) loneliness, poverty, social isolation that I do not relish. A 'single' status where everything is twice the cost. No other income to rely on other than what you generate yourself. No partner to share life's problems with or do anything for you. Single limited income to pay for maintenance and repairs.

Demographic trends in Western nations suggest that a rising share of unpartnered people will be entering retirement age in the near future. These may be the never married, widows and widowers or divorced people who have not re-partnered. There is clear evidence that singles living alone, particularly the never married, experience economic and health disadvantages in retirement. This is the case for both men and women. A major US review presents data to indicate that the never married have the largest share of persons aged 65 or over living in poverty (nearly 22 per cent), compared to 4.5 per cent of married persons, 17 per cent of the divorced and 14.5 per cent of widows/widowers. Singles living alone must rely on one income and do not have the benefits of pooling resources or economies of scale available to those sharing a household; for example it costs the same to heat a house regardless of how many live there.[8]

An example of this level of disadvantage is shown in a recent longitudinal study in which 1000 older citizens of Melbourne, Australia, were followed up for 16 years. At the beginning of the study, three-quarters of the sample said they wanted to stay in their homes, with help, when they could no longer cope with independent living. Only 5 per cent said they preferred to move to an aged care facility. However, after 16 years, 17 per cent had moved into such a facility, despite their preferences. Being single was a risk factor for non-preferential moving to an age care residence, as were being a woman, renting (that is, not owning your own home) and depression.[9]

Marriage and cohabitation proffer health advantages as well as financial benefits. Married people live longer on average than the unmarried, and never married men have particularly high mortality rates. For the over 65s, health-related restrictions on daily activities and physical inactivity rates are higher in the never married than the married, with rates for divorced and widowed people falling in between. Why is this so? Speculations include the idea of 'marriage protection' (marriage is associated with social approval and promotes healthier habits) and the 'marriage selection bias' (healthier people with more adaptive lifestyle habits are more likely to get married in the first place).

As is illustrated by the quotes at the beginning of this section, singles are also more likely to become socially isolated once they leave the workforce. Living alone is a risk factor, one that is exacerbated by health and financial limitations on activities. Of course, not all unmarried or never married people live alone, and not all those who live alone are lonely. Differences in temperament, family and friendship networks, and social opportunities all mitigate the risk of loneliness and isolation. For example, a group of single women retirees we are aware of have moved to apartments in the same building so they can assist each other as they age. They arrange regular outings and meals together but retain the privacy of their own living spaces. Others talk about the active efforts they have made to manage a satisfying retirement lifestyle as a single, as in the following example.

> I have several close friends who are also single and who retired around the same time as me, and therefore we have been a support for each other in some ways. I have always been very busy both in work and with life in general, I have always had a positive outlook on life, and I believe retirement is enabling me to focus more on my personal desires rather than workplace issues.

NEW INTIMACIES

As we have noted, singles, divorcees and widows/widowers may be particularly vulnerable to loneliness and social isolation when they retire. It is not surprising that new partnerships are sought or formed in these retirement years. An issue for retirees seeking intimate partners is that they are no longer as well connected to workplace networks, which usually provide opportunities to meet people. One solution is to go online.

Dating websites, apps or social media have proliferated in recent years, and older people, no less than young, see these as a means of finding companionship and romance. While some potential partners are genuine, there are those whose pretence of being a prospective companion is a ploy. Newspapers and other media abound with stories of retirees using these services who have been victims of fraud or scammed in some way. Victims report financial exploitation, pervasive lying and unwanted sexual aggression, among other negative experiences. So why do older women and men use these sites? Expanding their social networks, for friendship and romance and knowing more about one's partner are benefits of online dating reported by older dating site users. Scammers can play on triggers such as these to entice people to provide money, gifts or personal details. But sadly, as well as the financial price there is also an emotional cost for those looking for love online when the scam becomes evident. With appropriate care and safeguards, online dating and friendship sites may lead to the formation of successful and long-lasting relationships. Even if they do not fulfil this purpose, such sites offer the opportunity to meet interesting people and remain socially engaged, as long as they are approached with due caution. Not everyone met online is a scammer!

WORKPLACE SOCIALISING

Peer group socialising and friendships also undergo change when we retire. One of the functions of many workplaces is that they provide social connections. These can be quite extensive, including not just day-to-day interactions but a range of after-work social opportunities and events. In some cases, close friendships are formed, but even when this does not occur, there are usually people around in most workplaces to have a cup of coffee or a chat with. As well as colleagues, customers come and go during the day, providing interest and social interaction – someone to talk to and perhaps something to talk about. When we asked retirees what they missed most about work, many mentioned friends and colleagues.

> [I missed] being with work colleagues who are friends willing to listen and also to be listened to in supportive ways.

> I miss the camaraderie of my workmates.

Gender difference research suggests that men can feel more at a loose end socially in their retirement because, as we have noted previously, they are less likely than women to have developed social networks outside of the workplace. For example, Australian women perceive they have more friends to confide in, greater social support, more contact with their friends and family and lower levels of loneliness than men.[10] These social patterns are evident during working years and persist in retirement. One large survey of retirees indicated that retired women were more likely than retired men to spend time with family members, socialise with friends on a regular basis, volunteer within their community or provide care for another person – all socially based activities. Men were more likely than women to spend their retirement time in full-time or part-time work, staying engaged with aspects of their former career that they enjoyed, or involving themselves in sport. These activities can also include a social element, but it is more likely to be focussed around an activity and possibly less likely to engender intimacy and social support.[11]

Once you have retired it is more difficult to maintain relationships with workplace colleagues, who will still be busy during the working day. Close workplace friendships may suffer when there is not the opportunity to catch up on a daily basis, and special 'dates' or telephone calls cut into the family time of those still working. Many acquaintances and casual friendships will not be renewed. Of course, many retirees do maintain active friendships with former colleagues who become a strong part of their post-retirement social group. For most though, already existing non-work friendship circles will become more salient, and there will be a challenge to join new groups and make new friendships of fellow retirees. The challenge is likely to be greater for those who have been more committed to their workplace, worked longer hours, live alone and/or have fewer family connections. The risk of loneliness and social isolation, discussed below, is real.

SOCIAL CONNECTEDNESS AND LONELINESS

The headline of a recent article in the UK-based *Telegraph* newspaper, 'Wanted: Job for lonely widower (89) bored of retired life', is a poignant reminder of the extent to which loneliness can be a risk factor for the retired and elderly. With positive marital relationships one of the strongest protective factors against loneliness, the newly widowed are particularly vulnerable. What is missing from the lives of lonely people? A survey of over 65s by the UK's Campaign to End Loneliness found it was often those simple and ordinary interactions we too readily take for granted – like sitting with someone (52 per cent missed this), laughing with someone (missed by 51 per cent), having a hug (46 per cent) or sharing a meal (35 per cent). One 87-year old man described his loneliness as like a 'heavy cloud' hanging over him.[12]

A strong intimate partnership, higher education and income are protective factors against loneliness, as is personal temperament. Although events like widowhood can increase feelings of aloneness, on the whole this feeling does not change much throughout life. People who have never felt particularly lonely are more likely to eventually bounce back from setbacks like widowhood (which is, of course, not to underestimate its impact). The lonely widower in the newspaper article had already used some positive coping strategies to improve his life. Most importantly, he has asked for help and support.

Independent risk factors for loneliness include being male, physical health symptoms, chronic work and/or social stress, small social network, lack of a spousal confidant and poor quality social relationships.[13] Those who are ill or stressed have fewer resources to develop or maintain friendships; for example, they may lack mobility to visit others or attend clubs and interest groups. Smaller social networks are susceptible to further reduction as friends move location, become less mobile themselves as they age or eventually die. As we saw in a previous section, men's socialising is stereotypically more activity based and less intimate than women's, a style that means that men's friendship groups may be more susceptible to disbanding when life changes like retirement or the disabilities of ageing occur.

An important factor mitigating against loneliness is social connectedness. This has been described as having a sense of belongingness to a social group, a group in which there is trust, shared purpose and mutual obligation. Lack of social connectedness differs from loneliness, as it is possible to be socially connected to others yet still feel lonely or to be socially isolated yet contented. Nevertheless social isolation and loneliness are strongly related for most people. Many studies indicate the physical and psychological health benefits of social connectedness. It is a resilience factor that assists in coping with the ups and downs of day-to-day life, including the retirement transition and the changes of ageing. The socially connected experience more companionship, have more activity options to alleviate boredom and have a larger circle to call on in times of stress or trouble. A review of nearly 150 studies found that those who reported lower levels of social connection had a greater risk of early death than those who smoked, drank or were obese.[14] Although loneliness is a risk factor for poor health outcomes, some researchers have concluded that it is lack of social connectedness that is the more powerful factor.[15]

In one interesting study, a group of UK seniors was followed across the first six years of retirement. A questionnaire measured their social group membership and quality of life at retirement and again six years later. Mortality over the period of the study was monitored. Social group memberships of the sample ranged widely, including, for example, book clubs, sporting teams, trade unions and religious study groups. Retirees who were members of more social groups following their transition to retirement – and who retained these memberships post-retirement – had better quality of life and greater longevity than those with fewer or less long-lasting group membership. These patterns were not evident among a matched group of seniors who did not retire during the time of the study, suggesting to the authors that group membership had 'a distinct role to play in the process of adapting to new circumstances following retirement' (p. 6). What's more, these effects on both quality of life and longevity were comparable in size to those of physical activity, a well-established factor in maintenance of health during the senior years.[16]

Retiring from the workplace can certainly heighten the risk of losing social connectedness. A significant number of those retirees we surveyed reported that loneliness or social isolation were the worst aspects of retirement for them. As one said, 'At first I felt very isolated and lonely and all I wanted to do was curl up in a ball and cry'. This woman set to work on her social connections, joined several clubs in her area and turned her situation around, finally being able to say, 'I now have a new group of friends and am enjoying a great number of activities'.

Social isolation among seniors can negatively affect physical and mental health, increase mortality risk and contribute to cognitive decline. It can lead to retirees becoming more vulnerable to scams and other forms of elder abuse.[17] It is a clear health risk. What strategies can help to alleviate social isolation and its consequences?

OVERCOMING SOCIAL ISOLATION

Early in retirement, when you are more likely to be fit, healthy and energetic, is often a good time to work towards setting up new social networks to replace those lost or reduced as a result of leaving the workforce. You might arrange regular get-togethers with other retirees or former colleagues, increase your commitment to already existing friendship groups, join a club, take up a hobby that involves interacting with others or try one of the suggestions below.

Volunteering is one way to reduce loneliness among retirees, presenting as it does the opportunity to work with others toward a common and worthwhile goal, to make new friends and to increase social connections. Various clubs or organisations often combine group-based volunteering with social, sporting and educational activities. Many studies have shown that volunteering has positive physical and mental health benefits for older adults, for example, increased self-esteem, self-efficacy and life satisfaction, and even decreasing mortality. There is evidence that volunteering or 'civic engagement' partially offsets role losses encountered in later life, including the role losses that come about through retirement.[18]

Another strategy can be to access some of the many educational opportunities open to seniors. Taking classes in something you have always wanted to do or further developing a skill or knowledge base you already have is a great way to meet like-minded people. A review of studies looking at various types of interventions on senior loneliness found that the most effective programmes for combating isolation had an educational or training component: for instance, classes on health-related topics, computer training or exercise classes.[19] Group exercise classes for seniors are particularly effective and have the added bonus of increasing fitness and flexibility.

Getting a job is also a possibility for those who are still fit and healthy enough. As we have seen, these days retirement does not necessarily mean a 'cold turkey' approach to giving up work. Many retirees take on part-time or even full-time work for a period of time after retiring from their 'main' job or career. While helping to strengthen finances, this strategy can also be a way to build new friendships and develop new social roles.

Gender-based organisations such as the Men's Shed movement (based in the UK, Australia and parts of Europe) can be helpful to retired men who are missing their workplace-based social networks. The Men's Shed Movement is designed to promote physical and psychological health by strategies such as encouraging men to take advantage of medical checks available to seniors, providing information about health problems common to older males and working toward de-stigmatising mental illness, particularly depression. Local chapters are often based around a 'drop-in' casual model and tend to be informal and action-based, rather than talk-based, although group presentations on issues of interest are sometimes arranged. Men might be engaged in a variety of activities such as working on a carpentry project or fixing an old car, in groups or individually. The aim here is to appeal to men who enjoy company but don't necessarily self-identify as 'joiners'.

Facebook and other technology-based groups can provide ways to keep in touch for those who are isolated geographically or limited in their mobility. A caution is that over-reliance on technology for social contact can lead to further feelings of isolation if screen time is not followed up by face-to-face socialising, at least to some extent. Reputable online communities for seniors like Starts at 60 promote local meet-ups and other community activities that offer opportunities for socialising and making new friends in the 'real' world.

It doesn't work for everyone, but group-based living is another possible way to overcome social isolation. Some retirees move in with their children or other relatives to form multi-generational households. These offer many social and financial benefits, but can also strain family relationships if expectations are not mutual and boundaries not respected. Retirees who are single, widowed or divorced sometimes group together with like-minded friends to share housing or live in neighbouring apartments. Leisure activities, daily chores and expenses may be shared. When these situations work well, group members assist and support each other in difficult times, but again, it is important that all group members have clear expectations and contingencies, such as serious illness, have been thought through. Retirement villages are yet another form of group living that can provide social activities, connections and support for retirees. While many articles have been written about potential pitfalls of retirement villages (particularly financial issues), they clearly work well for some. Perhaps the major piece of advice that can be offered regarding a move to group living of any kind is to try before you buy, or buy into, any new arrangement to assess whether it suits you, and discuss any economic implications with a financial advisor or trusted friend.

Of course, strengthening your social connections does not have to involve a major life change like moving house. A dog or other pet can provide company, exercise and the chance to meet and chat to other humans through joining a club or just going for a walk. There is ample research that pet ownership is associated with greater wellbeing in older adults and that one of its effects is to mitigate loneliness.[20] For human company, some retirees join their workplace alumni associations and maintain contacts with former colleagues in that way. Others make a special effort to get to know their neighbours or follow up youthful friendships that they have let slide because of the pressures of work and family. Some simply enjoy having the time to commit to long-standing friendships and social groups. The key message here is that maintaining social contacts post-retirement is vital to health and wellbeing. For many, it will require purposive effort to guard against the unhealthy possibility of social isolation.

6

RE-SHAPING IDENTITY IN RETIREMENT

What do you do? It is a common conversation starter, signifying not only the social value of work, but the way in which one's job role is often viewed as a marker of social status and, quite possibly, attitudes to the world. Whether your response is doctor, teacher, clerk, mechanic or any other job or profession, the expectation is that you identify with the norms of that work role. Your job title tells people something about *you*, not just the job you do. It is part of your identity. So what message does 'I'm retired' give? In this chapter, we discuss the psychological re-adjustment to our sense of self that occurs during the retirement journey.

RETIREMENT AS AN IDENTITY DISRUPTER

What do we mean by psychological identity? A sense of identity has been described as having an understanding of who you are and what matters to you, of having some clarity about your life goals and purposes. In the developmental psychology literature, adolescence is considered the key life stage at which we develop an adequate sense of identity. Failure to do so results in the uncommitted apathy of role confusion. Pathways that include choice of, and success in, roles that are socially valued and purposeful provide the most normative route toward identity development. For adolescents, that typically means choosing a course of study, job or career that has personal meaning and leads toward a functional adult life. Theorists have postulated that an 'identity crisis' is a defining feature of adolescence, as young people struggle to find this direction in life.

By the time we get to our middle and senior years, identity is considered to be relatively stable and role confusion unlikely. We know who we are and where we are going, most of the time anyway. For many, if not most adults, a significant aspect of our identity relates to the work we do. Paid work is a key role in life, not only because of the number of hours we spend in this role. Jobs provide status and social feedback. Work also makes an important contribution to our sense of self by enabling us to take on other adult roles, such as providing for a family or being perceived as a responsible community member (rather than a 'lay-about' or 'dole cheat').

Some writers have suggested that retirement creates a new identity crisis. Is this true? It seems to be for some. While the core of a stable identity may well be an outcome of maturing from adolescent to adult, it is certainly true that any major life change can lead to questioning one's identity, with a consequent need to re-adjust and re-negotiate roles and life purposes. Marriage, parenthood, divorce, migration and retirement are all examples of such life changing events that will lead to modifications in one's sense of self, a process that may trigger anxiety and stress in some, excitement in others and a mix of emotions in most. As roles are added or lost, aspects of identity may be disrupted or strengthened to form a different and more complex whole. The extent to which there is psychosocial 'crisis' during this process is likely to depend on the size, nature and speed of the life change, the extent to which one was attached to the work role, one's temperament, the availability of social support and the extent to which other desirable roles are forthcoming. In previous chapters, we presented evidence to show that retirement satisfaction and adjustment are linked to many different variables, including the opportunity to plan and choose when to retire (Chapter 1) and the extent to which social support and connectedness is available to the retiree (Chapter 5). Let us now consider the influence of worker identity on managing the retirement transition.

WORKER IDENTITY AND RETIREMENT ADJUSTMENT

We asked participants in our large sample study of retired women, 'What do you miss most about working?' While many said 'nothing' or 'the money', a significant number of responses were couched in terms of the role of work in identity and meaning making.

> [I miss] feeling worthwhile. I think I'm of the generation who sees my value in terms of the job I do. I feel I have lost my identity.

> [I miss] the identity and recognition I received, and the sense of purpose/worth achieved by the challenges of work.

Others said 'I feel invisible', 'I've lost my sense of purpose' or 'I miss making a contribution'.

We also asked these women their reasons for working, giving them the opportunity to rate as 'very important', 'important' or 'not important', ten different work motives. Some reasons were considered stronger indicators of a tendency to shape personal identity around workplace activities and goals. These included acknowledging that work 'makes a contribution to my sense of who I am', 'contributes to my self-esteem', 'provides intellectual stimulation' and 'gives me a sense of making a contribution'. In our well-educated sample, a large percentage of respondents considered each of these reasons for working were very important (56, 52, 69 and 60 per cent respectively). We used these items to develop a measure of worker identity and found that those who had retired from occupations of professional and managerial status scored significantly higher on this aspect of identity than those who retired from occupations to which lower status was attached. Similarly, higher levels of education were associated with stronger worker identity. In these findings, we simply replicated a general consensus of organisational psychology research, that those in socially valued occupations and/or occupations that require longer and more committed training are more likely to view their work role as a significant aspect of their sense of self. This is true for both men and women.

We were able to examine how strength of worker identity was associated with adjustment to retirement, using a range of statistical techniques. As might have been predicted, those with stronger ties to their work role expressed less satisfaction with their retirement than those with weaker ties. This was a statistically significant effect, albeit a quite small one. There were many individual differences, even among the strongly work attached, in the extent to which dissatisfaction with retirement was expressed. For example, it depended to some extent on how long the women had been retired. Dissatisfaction was more likely to occur in those who had recently relinquished their paid work roles. Those retired for longer periods had more time to adjust and were consequently more comfortable with their role. Other factors which modified the effect of worker identity were number of activities participated in during retirement and satisfaction with social connectedness. Those who had taken on a larger variety of roles post-work, and those who perceived they were more socially connected, were more likely, in time, to overcome the negative feelings associated with the loss of their work role.

These are not surprising findings. The 'workaholic', those committed to their jobs and who spend long hours at work or thinking about it, have less time to develop responsibilities in the community, get to know their neighbours, maintain and nurture their friendships or enjoy hobbies and interests. They need time to process their change of status, experiment with new roles and channel their passions in new directions. As we saw in Chapter 2, retirement is a psychosocial journey, not simply a change of state.

Findings from previous research about the association between worker identity and retirement adjustment are equivocal. Some show a positive relationship of worker identity with retirement adjustment, while others, like ours, show a negative relationship.[1] This variation in outcomes is likely to be for at least two reasons. First, different outcome measures have been employed across different studies, for example self-esteem, retirement adjustment or life satisfaction. We found a negative effect of worker identity on retirement satisfaction, but no association with overall life satisfaction, indicating that worker identity does not necessarily have pervasive effects. A second issue is that there are so many factors influencing retirement adjustment and not all studies control for all of these. We found effects of worker identity diminished over time, and others have also shown that the longer you are retired, the less likely that the influences from your working days will affect current adjustment.[2] Other influences take over, such as strength of friendships and enjoyment of new activities.

A concept called 'older worker identity' has been postulated as influential in the ease or difficulty of adjusting to retirement. Older worker identity describes a set of self-beliefs regarding one's diminishing capacity, because of age, to successfully manage one's occupational tasks. Examples of items in an Older Worker Identity Scale include 'I am less effective in accomplishing my work', 'I have become less creative in accomplishing my work', 'I am no longer motivated to accomplish my tasks' and 'I have become less adaptable and flexible'.[3] Interestingly, while older worker identity relates to intention to retire in several studies, it has not been shown to improve retirement adjustment.[4] This may be because it comprises a quite negative set of beliefs about ageing and performance. Retiring because of feeling less able and competent imbues this stage of life with more negative overtones than retiring in order to achieve new goals.

GENDER DIFFERENCES

Early studies of retirement adjustment concluded that men had more difficulties in managing this transition than women, because their occupational attachments (or worker identities) were stronger and because they had weaker social networks and fewer 'non-work routines' (by which was meant domestic and community duties).[5] Such research does not take into account the strong growth in women's employment in the last 20 to 50 years or of women's improved representation in higher status jobs. More recently there have been some suggestions that it is women who will find the transition more difficult because they are likely to retire having achieved fewer work goals (including financial security) than men. This postulated state of affairs is said to be a result of women's typical work patterns, which involve breaks in employment and generally lower status jobs.

Although there is no shortage of commentary and opinion on possible gender differences in both worker identity and retirement adjustment, up-to-date evidence is sparse. One qualitative interview study of retirees (22 men and 26 women) aged 50 to 65 years found 'traditional gender roles predominated', with men more likely to experience negative emotions on retirement and more likely to have viewed their work role as central to their identity. For example, one man described how he felt identity loss, anger and a diminution of his (and his family's) status in the community when he was made redundant, even though he was financially secure, able to find bridging employment and had many interests outside work. While these reactions were more common among the men, some women experienced them as well, for example one female teacher who was constrained to retire at 60 likened her feelings to a grief reaction, a kind of bereavement for a lost self. Nevertheless, the study authors concluded that because of the predominance of traditional gender roles among the sample, the men they interviewed found the transition to retirement more difficult, as it stripped away an important aspect of what they perceived to be their masculine identity. Home-based, domestic roles and leisure pursuits did not adequately compensate for this loss.[6]

In a recent qualitative study, 34 male professional engineers aged 55 to 77 years were interviewed to talk about their late-stage career development.[7] Although not specifically asked about retirement, many spoke of it, mostly using negative language, such as 'problem' or 'trouble'. They foresaw financial worries, social isolation (going from 'talking to 60 people a day to talking to the cat'), a lack of other interests to fill their time, fear of ageing ('closing the gate, being put out to pasture') and significantly, loss of identity ('I will no longer have the voice my position gives me'; 'You still seem to need something that preserves your worth'). In the later stages of their careers, these engineers had shaped their identities around being wise elders and knowledge custodians, people of purpose and value. They struggled with a belief that ageing and retirement would negate their contributions and thus, their worth as a person. A sense of indignation, and to some extent fear of the future, was palpable ('They wash their hands of you . . .').

A couple of studies have focused on retired professional women, possibly to ascertain whether they have similar difficulties to work-identified men through the retirement journey. In one such study, 14 retired professional women, aged 64 to 82 years and who had retired between seven and 15 years ago, were each interviewed twice. The aim was to examine how these women managed their retirement transition, particularly their process of renegotiating identity and life roles.[8] Several reflected on how they had experienced 'rolelessness' when they first retired and had initially struggled to find new life purposes. However the majority of the women did not report continuing disruption to their sense of self or identity. One woman nicely encapsulated this general finding:

> I always thought of myself as a person, as not just an occupation. Some people, they are an occupation and that's it. But ah, I had enough things that I was interested in and wanted to do that it didn't change.[9]

The women adopted three strategies to maintain the integrity of their self-concepts. First, they expressed strong, often multifaceted, pre-retirement self-concepts. Several noted the importance of their non-work roles, such as family, community and friendship roles. Second, 13 of the 14 women continued to practise their professional skills in one way or another post-retirement. They stated or implied that this continuity helped maintain their sense of competence. Finally, many of the study participants emphasised the value of discovering new skills and interests once retirement allowed them the time to do so. In fact, all the women had practised 'role expansion', substituting the loss of their professional roles with alternative roles such as volunteer work, board membership, mentoring or part-time/casual work in their previous field (for example as a substitute teacher).

While the women in this study were aware of identity disruption as a potential outcome of retirement from their professional occupations, they took active steps to maintain a robust sense of self through both holding on to aspects of their pre-retirement personas and embracing new opportunities to expand their roles and goals. Very similar findings emerged from another small, in-depth interview study of professional women, which found that when these women retired, they engaged in psychological 'work' to re-negotiate new identities as retirees. Strategies included the carry-over of key elements of worker identity into retirement (for example sense of competence), developing new roles through volunteering and helping others, continuing to learn new skills and focusing on the nurture of social networks.[10]

It seems there is a need for further research on the role of gender in retirement adjustment. First, there is a research gap in examining the characteristics and identity-restructuring strategies used by men who are successful, satisfied retirees. Second, replication of some of the early large-scale gender difference studies is needed to reflect the modern day working environment of (somewhat) greater equality between the sexes.

ONCE A WORKER, ALWAYS A WORKER?

In this chapter so far, we have discussed how one's sense of identity can be disrupted by leaving behind the worker role and how that disruption can have effects on retirement adjustment. We have described some of the strategies that retirees use to redefine themselves and modify their identities as retired persons. In this section, we step back a bit with the reminder that worker identity can, and often does, remain a significant and healthy part of retiree self-definition. For example, in answering the question we posed at the beginning of the chapter, 'What do you do?', many retirees will answer, 'I'm a retired teacher/doctor/manager/electrician'. This self-description often goes beyond simply naming a past role, it implies something about present retirement activities. The next part of such a self-description is likely to fall into one of two categories. The first is an explanation of how the old role has been incorporated into the new, for example, 'I'm a retired teacher still doing casual teaching/volunteering as an English language teacher for new migrants/setting up a tutoring business'. The second is an explanation of how the old role has been left behind and a new, different role has taken its place, for example, 'I'm a retired teacher who is now an art student/who's setting up a travel agency/who is writing a novel about space ships'.

As retirement researchers Reitzes and Mutran put it, 'Retirees still think of themselves in terms of their former careers. Even when they no longer occupy the role, their identity lingers'.[11] Sense of self in retirement is forged from a mix of new and old roles.

A Swiss study of 792 persons aged 58 to 70 years, 443 of whom had retired and 349 who had not done so, addresses this issue of lingering worker identity.[12] A major aim was to examine how retired people's self-image differs from that of workers'. Participants were asked to rate the importance of different self-description domains such as professional and family roles. Results indicated that the professional domain remained just as important for self-description to retirees as it was for those still working. In general, retired respondents were more 'identity diverse', rating more domains of self-description as important than did the not-yet-retired respondents. No domain of self-description became less important after retirement. Additionally, high identity diversity correlated with high life satisfaction. The more roles seniors assessed as important to them, the happier they were, either as workers or retirees.

There are various strategies that retirees use to maintain the salience of their worker identity. Which ones are deemed most attractive by retirees will depend on the type of job and the type of workplace from which they retired. For example, home-based workers in retirement might still occasionally accept a paid or unpaid contract, but may be less likely to attend social events associated with their former career.

Those who found a high level of intellectual stimulation in their former occupation are more likely to keep reading about progress and process in that field than those who were less cognitively involved. In our own study, the most common strategies used were reading about developments and changes in one's former field or place of work (41 per cent did this often, 45 per cent sometimes) and maintaining friendships with former work colleagues (34 per cent often, 49 per cent sometimes). About one-quarter of participants maintained links through attending social events (such as Christmas parties) at their former workplace, approximately 20 per cent went to talks or meetings associated with the field in which they had worked and a similar proportion continued active membership of their professional association or union. A greater number, about 36 per cent, sometimes or often continued to do unpaid work in their area of expertise, for example mentoring or giving talks, while 18 per cent were casually employed in paid work from time to time. In short, retirees maintained work identity through both informal social links and more formal structural links; they utilised skills and contacts gained over their working life in contributing to their new identities.[13]

We measured 'workplace attachment' by combining participant ratings on the items described above to form a scale and examined the associations between scale scores and several other variables. We found that those with professional or managerial jobs, or stronger worker identities before they retired, not surprisingly, had higher workplace attachment scores post-retirement. Workplace attached retirees were more highly educated and more active, in the sense that they engaged in a greater range of social and leisure pursuits than those who were less inclined to keep alive the links with their former occupations. Finally, they were more generative, expressing a greater satisfaction with their lifetime social and community contributions. It seems that workplace attachment strategies provided a path toward negotiating the retirement transition.

Workplace attachment declined as length of retirement increased (and people aged). This tendency was reflected in the way workplace attachment related to overall satisfaction with life. Those who were more workplace attached were generally more satisfied, but this only applied to the first 10 years of retirement. Retirees – even those who strongly maintain their worker identity through continuing links with their workplace and/or former career – tend to gradually replace these links or let them drop out over time, without diminution of general satisfaction. Presumably, other (or fewer) activities replace workplace contacts and interests.

MANY PATHWAYS

As we noted earlier in the chapter, worker identity is stronger among those in professional and higher status occupations. It is also likely to be stronger for those who have not, in their working life, maintained what is often termed a 'work/life balance'. However, those who 'work to live' rather than 'live to work' are also likely to structure their sense of self in part around the roles that paid work provides, for example a contributor to social order, a breadwinner, a friendly colleague, a union member. On retirement, adjustments to these roles, and therefore sense of self, will still be required. They will be different for the neurosurgeon and the council worker, the teacher and the prison guard, the home-based IT worker and the manager of a large corporation, but they will be adjustments nonetheless.

Post-retirement psychological re-adjustments can involve maintenance and adaptation of one's worker identity in ways that have been discussed already in this chapter. But re-shaping worker identity is only one of the pathways to the re-establishment of identity in retirement. For some, it is not an option because retirement will mean severing of most or all ties with the workplace. For some it will not be desirable because they neither enjoyed their work nor found it fulfiling. That being so, retirement still offers many satisfying opportunities for renewal, such as allowing the time to focus on new and already established interests and hobbies, give back to the community, strengthen family ties or work through a 'bucket list' of desired activities.

Pathways to re-shaping identity can and do take many directions, and are likely to include periods of experimentation with some successes and some failures. Not all new activities and roles tried out will be sustained, not all friendship overtures will be fulfiling. Nevertheless, research is strong on the importance of social connectedness and the maintenance of social roles for retirement wellbeing (see Chapter 5). Developmental psychologists theorise that generative roles will be the most rewarding in one's middle and senior years, and that these will contribute to a stronger and more contented sense of self. These are roles that involve giving back to the community (for example through volunteering), fostering personal creativity or investing in future generations (for example through mentoring the young or caring for grandchildren). While worthy, these roles are not available to all. No doubt a significant proportion of retirees are satisfied to shape a new identity around relaxation, leisure and social contact, to 'be' rather than constantly need to 'do'.

7

MAKING THE MOST OF RETIREMENT

So much to do, so little time, or so much time, so little to do? Which is it to be?

For some of us the onset of retirement can create anxiety because we don't know what to expect. What will life look like when work no longer consumes the majority of our waking hours, and how we will define ourselves when our job is no longer a key part of our identity? What should retirement look like, and how should we be spending our time?

Over two decades ago, Betty Frieden[1] coined the term 'human work' to describe the unique opportunities available in retirement. Human work refers to the tasks, however large or small, that we choose freely, and that we do out of love rather than obligation. As one writer puts it, 'Human work is a good term because it honours ageing – and retirement – in all its diversity and complexity'.[2] It also raises awareness of the many possibilities for psychological growth in ageing and old age.

As we have seen in previous chapters, how we develop in retirement is influenced by a complex set of factors, including our histories, our personalities, our feelings about ourselves and our relationship to work. Some retirees have worked at jobs in which they felt powerless in the face of institutional policies and practices over which they had no control. Those who have endured long hours at difficult jobs that took a physical and psychological toll might choose to spend retirement, at least in the early years, in peace and quiet. Retirement for them brings blessed relief from the stresses of work. On the other hand, those for whom work was challenging and growth enhancing might choose to pursue connections with work in retirement, although in different degrees and intensities, or to seek activities which they may have had to defer such as new and stimulating leisure pastimes. So what is 'good' retirement for one is not necessarily 'good' retirement for another. And, of course, retirement may mean different things to the next generations of retirees, for whom work patterns may be more and more centred on working from home and on flexible working hours, perhaps resulting in less connection to a fixed workplace. Not to mention the increasing presence of robots taking over many work functions!

How can today's retirees make the most of retirement? In thinking about this question we need to take note of the close relationship between ageing and retirement. While retirement ages may differ considerably, this stage of life is inescapably bound up with the ageing process and the normal changes over this period. Retirees must face the usual health problems of getting older, as well as the social, psychological and economic consequences of this life stage.

In this last chapter we have chosen not to provide specific summaries of topics covered in earlier chapters. Rather, we focus in more general terms on how to spend retirement in ways that are satisfying and growth promoting and how to plan for this. We also canvass some of the regrets that were expressed by retired women in our own study. These resonate with comments from the many retired men and women we have talked to and what we have noted from the literature.

WHAT CONTRIBUTES TO 'SUCCESSFUL' RETIREMENT?

Previous chapters have detailed the many facets of retirement that contribute to wellbeing and satisfaction during this stage of life. It is not our intention to rehearse these here; rather we focus on one other important part of the retired life, namely the activities retirees engage in.

> I am so happy in retirement, far more than I expected. I feared boredom and loss of meaning, but it's been easy to find so many worthwhile activities that I've never been busier. As so many others say: 'How did I ever find time to fit in work?' – it's so true. . . . I've been able to study for sheer pleasure and interest, and I've been able to travel. As someone said to me recently: 'You live the life we all aspire to'. What's not to love?

No longer regarded as the end of life, retirement can be considered as a next life stage in which activities delayed by full-time work can be pursued and new life choices made. It is an opportunity to engage at last in those pursuits that matter most to each individual. The most common retirement activities people plan to pursue when they retire include travel, engaging in hobbies of various sorts, gardening, sport, getting fit through exercise, reading and relaxing, home renovations and volunteering. Does the reality match these plans?

Yes it does, although there are gender differences. Women are less likely than men to be engaged in organised sport, monitor financial investments, work part-time or stay engaged with their pre-retirement occupation through reading, interest groups or meetings. Men volunteer less than women, and when they do join up as volunteers it is more likely in a supervisory role than as an 'on the ground' helper. Overall, women's retirement activities tend to be more social than men's, for example spending time with friends and caring for others. In our study, the most common activities women reported were reading, watching TV and listening to music while home-related activities were also usual. In another study, exercising and keeping fit were important for many women who described exercise classes as being an 'organising' element in their day, structured and scheduled, much like work had been.

There is considerable evidence that leisure activities make a positive contribution to retirement adjustment, life satisfaction and wellbeing.[3] Recognition of this comes in the many magazines, online and in print, available to retirees and seniors that urge readers to be active, with suggestions as to how this may be achieved. Our research showed that the more women engaged in activities, the more satisfied they were with retirement and with life in general. Satisfaction with retirement and with life was also predicted by many specific activities, especially travel, spending time with friends, 'get fit' activities, attendance at clubs and engaging in hobbies. Not surprisingly perhaps, satisfaction was not predicted by domestic chores or caring for others.

One question of interest is whether retirees typically take on new activities or retain old ones. In fact, some activities may have to be abandoned because of loss of physical capacity or energy or changing life circumstances. In these cases, retirement may act as an opportunity to begin new pursuits. We know that after retirement there is both continuity (maintaining pre-retirement activities) and disengagement (letting go of pre-retirement activities), but there has been little evidence available about the development of new interests and skills post-retirement. One small study of men and women who were highly engaged in leisure activities prior to retirement found that women were more innovative than men in their retirement leisure pursuits, while men tended to continue in their lifelong activities. Women tended to add more leisure roles after retirement rather than eliminate them.[4] The researchers concluded that for women, the impetus to add new leisure roles was not retirement itself but their liberation from gender role responsibilities that had previously defined their lives. Why men and women do and do not acquire new skills in retirement is a topic ripe for further research. Are gender differences in activities the result of early socialisation and gender roles? Are there differences in the opportunities available for men and women?

WHAT ARE THE REGRETS?

We were interested to find that the participants in our study had a great deal to say about difficulties they faced in their transition to retirement. After many years of structured daily life at work, the lack of structure may lead to a feeling of aimlessness and a corresponding erosion of wellbeing. As one of retired women in our study said:

> Adjusting to retirement is a slow process; in the beginning I had difficulty filling in my days and did not feel I was contributing much as a person.

Difficulties can be exacerbated when a partner is involved, as we have seen in Chapter 5. Although partnered individuals are more satisfied in retirement than unpartnered ones, for some the feeling of living out of each other's pockets can become overwhelming. It can take time to adjust. Another common problem is that the goals and desires of one partner can be sidelined in order to accommodate those of the other partner, who may or may not be retired. A plan for what you can and want to achieve in retirement will help avoid these problems. Don't wait until you actually retire. If you have a partner, talk to him/her about mutual (and single) activities. Two women in our study expressed it this way when asked what they might have changed about retirement:

> It would have been valuable if my partner and I had had (or still should have) more of a discussion on what my retirement might mean for us both together and individually. At times it feels as if our arrows are not pointing in the same direction as he is younger than me and not yet psychologically ready to retire.

> [I would] consider my needs over those of my husband. He retired some 10 years before I did and has been eager to take off to do the 'grey nomad' thing for many years now. Because he waited, somewhat impatiently, for me to finish doing my thing, I now feel under pressure to grant him his wish to take off on a whim. This makes it nigh on impossible for me to commit to the volunteer work that I feel I can, and should/would like, to do. I still have a great need to feel productive and useful, which now I do not have. It is a source of great conflict and unhappiness in our house.

Many retirees wish they had planned better for the free time that retirement brings; this was a strong focus among those we studied. While the benefits of retirement planning, especially financial planning, are well recognised, not all felt this way. One woman reminded us that there can be a downside to planning and life does not always follow an anticipated path.

> Sometimes life throws curveballs. No amount of planning can prepare a person for curveballs. The ability to remain flexible, resourceful and true to yourself is key to being able to survive them. Planning my retirement would not have helped me with regard to unexpected violence and trauma . . . the only thing that helped has been to have faith that good people will come into your life and support you through that transition as best as possible. The danger in 'planning' is it sets up 'expectations'.

Many comments referred to the benefit of a gradual move into retirement via part-time work where possible, thereby offering the opportunity to decide what they wanted to achieve post-retirement and plan accordingly.

> I think working part time leading to retirement would have been advantageous. So would seeing what volunteer options were available and trying them out on non-working days. Having said that, working part time in my job wasn't an option.

The concept of flexible work is not new and many companies offer it in some form – job sharing, telecommuting, compressed workweeks and part-time schedules. But such programmes are usually small in scale and, in practise, are largely taken up by those with family commitments. And often employees who participate pay a penalty; they see their careers suffer for it or retire with less financial security, as we have seen in our earlier discussion of women's often fragmented working lives. If companies offer flexibility programmes that are easily accessible to older workers and structure these so that people who participate don't feel that they're being sidelined there is a two-way benefit. The employer retains the skills and experience of older people, and the employee is able to move into full-time retirement at his or her own pace.

Regret at retiring early, either voluntarily or involuntarily, was not uncommon. We have noted the advantages and disadvantages of early retirement in several earlier chapters, with financial outcomes being one of the most problematic. Similarly, for those whose retirement timing is determined by others, the opportunities for planning may be limited and, as we have seen, these retirees may find themselves less satisfied with retirement than those who retire at a time of their choosing.

Finally on planning, one woman told us:

> If there'd been a program you could do to really think through what retirement would mean – what I'd lose and what I'd gain – so I could be better prepared, I would have done that.

Interestingly, a search of the internet found a great concentration on pre-retirement financial planning programmes although, presumably, many of these would also provide information on other key aspects of retirement. Such a pre-retirement programme, from our perspective, would include information (and homework!) on our four 'pillars' of retirement life – finance/housing, health, social relationships and identity/purpose. Earl[5] suggests businesses can help prepare their employees for retirement by providing access to pre-retirement planning and by thinking about retirement as part of a career development process, that is encouraging where possible a gradual move to part-time work if this is desired. The Australian Bureau of Statistics reports about 40 per cent of Australians want to work part time before permanently leaving the workforce, but their goal is not met by action. The main reason for this is fear of what their employer will think if they ask for part-time work and the readiness of employers to embrace this staged retirement. Clearly, the most effective programmes are those that discuss further employment possibilities and, as well, cover our four pillars of retirement life.

PLAN FOR A POSITIVE RETIREMENT

So how do we ensure a smooth transition to retirement? We need to spend just as much time thinking about what we need and want from our retirement as we spend planning for it financially. While each person's needs will differ, there are some common ways in which good planning can help establish good retirement.

As we have seen in Chapter 5, maintaining or establishing social connections is a key factor in 'successful' retirement. For many people, the work environment is one important source of friends and social contacts. While retirement does not necessarily mean these connections are lost, it does require some effort in seeking out old and finding new friends whether through a part-time job, clubs or any type of organised social activities. Staying active is another important element in healthy retirement, either through organised sports or activities, taking long walks, gardening or having the grandchildren for the day. There are many 'get fit' groups that offer older people the opportunity to strengthen their bodies and stave off ill health. Getting out of your comfort zones and into a new environment can do you good as well as spark new interests. If you have a partner, try to plan retirement activities together; communicate openly about issues that may arise as you transition to retirement.

Creative pursuits also fulfil retirement social and intellectual needs for many retirees. Opportunities abound to try out new creative activities, or extend commitment in pre-existing hobbies, through the plethora of classes and interest groups now available to seniors, many of them free or low cost. One mental exercise that has been suggested for those who are not sure what would interest them is to reflect back on what you enjoyed as a child. Often it is these activities that will re-awaken enthusiasm in later life. Examples include painting, craft, model making and creative writing.

Importantly, plan your retirement financial needs. How much do you think you will need after you stop paid work? At age 65 the average lifespan is 86; at age 85, the expectation is 92. 'The longer you live, the longer you are likely to live' with women living longer than men. The post-retirement lifespan has been conceptualised by some authors as having three health-related stages: disability-free years, years with some disability and dependent years. Quite clearly, the cost of retirement during these stages will differ and the last stage is going to be significantly more costly than the first two for most retirees. So careful planning is essential to ensure that you have adequate finances at this point in your life. But also consider how you spend your funds early in retirement in order to get the most out of this period of your life. Is drawing down on superannuation or other savings to fund travel or other life circumstances the best way to use your funds? Is downsizing into smaller or different accommodation the best option for you? These are the sorts of questions that we rarely address early in retirement, but the answers we choose may have great bearing on our later financial security.

BEING POSITIVE

The relatively new sub-discipline of positive psychology has examined the ways and means in which positive thinking influences health and happiness.[6] Flowing from this approach there are new research centres for positive ageing springing up in universities with a remit to find solutions to some of the key challenges facing an ageing population, including mobility, isolation and loneliness, changing spousal relationships, workforce participation and sexual health, among other issues. These centres are often focused on how society perceives and promotes positive ageing and wellbeing. Their aims are to change the negative perceptions we have of ageing and the competencies of the aged, and to encourage communities to develop supportive environments for healthier ageing.

Husband-and-wife authors, Patricia Edgar and Don Edgar, argue in *Peak, Reinventing Middle Age*[7] that middle age can be the apex of our lives, a time in which we capitalise on all we have experienced and learnt. They suggest that increased longevity means that all of us need to rethink our responsibility for looking after ourselves and contributing to society beyond our 50s and 60s. It's a very optimistic book, using recent research to explore opportunities and blockers to productive ageing, and the mini biographies that form the second part of the book show that flexibility in the later years can be the key to embracing a satisfying lifestyle. Research into longevity shows clearly that those who age successfully have enjoyed fulfiling lives. They have used their later years well, continuing a 'purposeful' life and being resilient in times of hardship. As the authors note,

> [S]ome aspects of ageing well are negotiable. The sooner we pay attention to them the better the outcome. The successful middle-aged are generally self-motivated and community-minded, manage their routines and their needs independently, and, although lonely from time to time, most are not isolated. They are not consumed by regrets and have learned to live day by day, remaining interested and interesting. Throughout their lives they have felt loved and worthwhile.[8]

We know that wellbeing is tied to having meaning and purpose in life, to having a reason to get out of bed for every day. There are many ways to achieve this, and individuals will have different methods of doing so. Staying fit and healthy after retirement is one way to maintain the quality of our life. It is true that the less we do, the less we will be able to do. A key to staying healthy is to eat well. To do this one needs to know and follow recommended dietary choices as we have seen in an earlier chapter. Having enough good quality sleep is fundamental for wellbeing. When we're tired it makes these other factors, such as getting exercise, eating well and finding meaning in life, much more difficult.

Importantly, research reveals that our attitude to life has a great impact on our emotions. We know that a positive attitude is correlated with happiness, health and better relationships. For older people their attitude to ageing is significant. Viewing ageing as a negative process is correlated with poorer outcomes than those who view age more positively and focus more on what they can do rather than what they can't. This is particularly so when dealing with the inevitable illnesses, aches and pains of old age.

We have seen in an earlier chapter that having a sense of connectedness to people and the community is vital for maintaining a positive attitude to retirement whereas loneliness and isolation is associated with poor outcomes. There is a need to actively protect oneself against isolation and there are many ways to do that: keep in touch with old friends, join local clubs, volunteer for an organisation, start and continue hobbies, enrol in a new course and so on. Retirement is a time when you can experiment with different activities. You have the time, and after a lifetime of experiences your self-esteem is robust enough to deal with a few mistakes and the occasional failures.

Finally, our research with grandparents[9] showed us how important laughter and play are for wellbeing. Many told us that this was one of the best aspects of grandparenting – the ability (and willingness) to discover their inner child and to throw themselves into fun behaviour. This sense of playfulness was regarded by grandparents as one of the best features of their interactions with grandchildren. It is not hard to imagine that this positive attitude might be part of an adaptive approach to life more generally, for example in keeping connected to younger generations and the very different lives they lead. As Dr Happy notes, losing that sense of play can easily lead to a dull, humdrum existence that can be hard to overcome. Finding something to laugh at – such as a funny movie – can be very therapeutic.

Take the opportunity to help reframe existing negative attitudes towards growing older. The belief that ageing is a process of inevitable decline does not necessarily reflect reality as we have seen in earlier chapters. If we think old we become old! An unsourced comment in a talk by George Carlin, American stand-up comedian, about old age[10] sums it up well:

> None of us are getting out of here alive, so please stop treating yourself like an afterthought. Eat the delicious food. Walk in the sunshine. Jump in the ocean. Say the truth that you're carrying in your heart like hidden treasure. Be silly, be kind, be weird. There's no time for anything else.

What will make you happy in your retirement? Do you love to socialise with friends? Do you love being with your grandchildren? Do you want to travel, perhaps become a 'grey nomad'? Do you want to commune with nature – in the garden or on long walks in the country? Do you want to spend this period of your life giving back to your community? There are many, many options for you to remain engaged, as busy as you want to be and fulfiled. You could also consider growing old disgracefully – doing things that may seem out of character, perhaps a bit 'naughty', not quite approved of by society. The choices you make will, of course, be determined by many factors, chief among these being your health and your financial state. But don't let these choices be determined by society or by your own sense of what is achievable.

FURTHER READING

SCHOLARLY ARTICLES

Barbosa, L. M., Monteiro, L., & Giardini Murta, S. (2016). Retirement adjustment predictors: A systematic review. *Work, Aging and Retirement*, 2(2), 262–280.
A systematic literature review concerning factors relating to adjustment to retirement (covering years 1995–2014).

Boyle, F., & Thomson, C. (2016). Establishing an evidence base for adapting social housing for an ageing population. *Journal of Financial Management of Property and Construction*, 21(2), 137–159.
Examines existing social housing stock in the UK and discusses how it relates to the needs of an ageing population.

Calvo, E., Sarkisian, N., & Tamborini, C. R. (2013). Causal effects of retirement timing on subjective physical and emotional health. *The Journals of Gerontology. Series B, Psychological Sciences and Social Sciences*, 68(1), 73–84.
A study of early, late and 'on time' retirement, with argument presented for introduction of later retirement ages.

Evans, S., Atkinson, T., Darton, R., Cameron, A., Netten, A., Smith, R., & Porteus, J. (2017). A community hub approach to older people's housing. *Quality in Ageing & Older Adults*, 18(1), 20–32.
Analysis of benefits, barriers and facilitators of community hub housing for retired and older individuals.

Fisher, G. G., Chaffee, D. S., & Sonnega, A. (2016). Retirement timing: A review and recommendations for future research. *Work, Aging and Retirement*, 2(2), 230–261.

Excellent, comprehensive review of research on retirement timing. The authors identify and discuss key factors that moderate the relation between retirement timing and consequences.

van der Heide, I., van Rijn, R. M., Robroek, S. W., Burdorf, A., & Proper, K. I. (2013). Is retirement good for your health? A systematic review of longitudinal studies. *BMC Public Health*, 13(1), 1–22.

A methodologically strong review of longitudinal studies examining mental and physical health effects of retirement among white collar and blue collar workers.

Vo, K., Forder, P. M., Tavener, M., Rodgers, B., Banks, E., Bauman, A., & Byles, J. E. (2015). Retirement, age, gender and mental health: Findings from the 45 and up study. *Aging & Mental Health*, 19(7), 647–657.

Large scale study of relationships between psychological distress, retirement and reasons for retirement.

Wang, M., & Shi, J. (2014). Psychological research on retirement. *Annual Review of Psychology*, 65, 209–233.

A review of the literature on the psychology of retirement over the past two decades (up to 2014).

Zantinge, E. M., van den Berg, M., Smit, H. A., & Picavet, H. J. (2014). Retirement and a healthy lifestyle: Opportunity or pitfall? A narrative review of the literature. *European Journal of Public Health*, 24(3), 433–439.

Review of literature and discussion of whether retirement is likely to be associated with adoption of healthier lifestyle.

BOOKS

Allen, C., Bearg, N., Foley, R., & Smith, J. (2015). *The retirement boom: An all inclusive guide to money, life, and health in your next chapter*. Wayne, NJ: Career Press.

A 'how to' guide to retirement, based on extensive interviews with workers and retirees. Topics include how to make your money last, renegotiating home life relationships, improving and maintaining health, building and leaving a legacy, simplifying your life.

Coon, A., & Feuerhern, J. (2017). *Thriving in retirement: Lessons from baby boomer women.* Santa Barbara, CA: Praeger.

One of the few resources that focuses on retirement for females, this book presents issues of relevance to retired women professionals from the baby boomer generation. It includes case material and insights into successful coping with this life stage.

Edgar, P., & Edgar, D. (2017). *Peak: Reinventing middle age.* Melbourne, Australia: Text Publishing Co.

Redefines the years from 50 to 75 as productive and active. Emphases the social and economic contributions made by this group, who no longer fit the 'old' stereotypes of yesteryear. Includes short biographies of people who have 'embraced their middle age in a variety of interesting and inspirational ways'.

Farrell, C. (2014). *Unretirement: How baby boomers are changing the way we think about work, community, and the good life.* London: Bloomsbury

The author argues that old ideas of retirement – opting out and winding down – are out-dated. He notes that the baby boomer generation is already extending their working lives with later retirement ages, new careers, voluntary services and entrepreneurial ventures. People are 'unretiring' because they recognise the economic, social and personal value of work.

Friedan, B. (1993). *The fountain of age.* New York, NY: Simon and Schuster.

In her classic book, Betty Friedan explores the positive aspects of ageing, examining the possibilities of new intimacies, purposes and self-discoveries. She talks about embracing a lifestyle that allows for personal growth rather than emphasising bodily decline.

FILMS

About Schmidt (New Line Cinema).

A 'grumpy old retiree' travels to his estranged daughter's wedding, in a journey that also turns out to be a voyage of self-discovery.

The Best Exotic Marigold Hotel (20th Century Fox).

British retirees travel to India to take up residence in what they believe is a newly restored hotel. Their retirement 'new start' does not turn out as expected, but each of the diverse characters grows as a person through their pleasures, difficulties and interactions.

The Intern (Warner Bros. Pictures).

Seventy-year-old widower Ben Whittaker is bored with his retirement. He takes up an opportunity to become a 'senior intern' at an online fashion company, run and staffed by people half his age. Youth and age learn from each other in mutually beneficial ways.

WEBSITES

AgeUK (www.ageuk.org.uk/leics/information-and-advice/useful-websites/).
Directory of websites aimed at older people.

Eldercare (US) (www.eldercare.gov/eldercare.NET/Public/index.aspx).
Connects people to services for older adults and their families. Includes a listing of federal websites that offer information on a range of critical eldercare issues.

Retirement Matters (UK) (www.retirement-matters.co.uk/).
This provides information on retirement related products and services including travel, finance and legal, health and lifestyle.

Starts at Sixty (StartsatSixty.com) and *Your Life Choices* (yourlifechoices.com.au).
These provide information regarding health, lifestyle, property, money, technology, entertainment, food and drink, travel and games. Also provide opinion pieces, current articles and trending topics that may be of interest to older people.

UK government retirement website (www.gov.uk/plan-retirement-income).
This provides information on planning retirement income.

US government retirement website (www.usa.gov/retirement).
This provides basic information about retirement and pension benefits in the US.

In addition, most governments have formal websites that provide information about financial matters, access to aged care and other issues for retirees and older citizens.

NOTES

CHAPTER 1

1 Office for National Statistics (UK). (2015). *How has life expectancy changed over time?* Retrieved from http://visual.ons.gov.uk/how-has-life-expectancy-changed-over-time/

2 Office for National Statistics (UK). (2016). *National life tables: 2013–2015.* Retrieved from www.ons.gov.uk/peoplepopulationandcommunity/birthsdeathsand marriages/lifeexpectancies/bulletins/nationallifetablesunitedkingdom/ 20132015

3 Wikipedia. (2017). *Retirement age.* Retrieved from https://en.wikipedia.org/ wiki/Retirement_age;

   Cutler, D. M., Meara, E., & Richards-Shubik, S. (2011, November). *Healthy life expectancy: Estimates and implications for retirement age policy.* Research Report. Retrieved January 29, 2017, from www.nber.org/aging/rrc/papers/ orrc10-11.pdf;

   Forette, F., Salord, J.-C., & Brieu, A.-M. (undated). *Living longer, working longer: A French challenge.* Research Report. Retrieved January 29, 2017, from www. ilc-alliance.org/images/uploads/publicationpdfs/Article_living_longer_ working_longer.pdf

4 *Australian advertising slogan aimed at retirees.* Retrieved from www.sunsuper.com.au/ thedreamproject/retirement-is-the-new-promotion

5 Moore, S. M., & Rosenthal, D. A. (2017). *Australian women in retirement survey.* Final Research Report. Unpublished document available from the authors.

6 Wang, M., & Shi, J. (2014). Psychological research on retirement. *Annual Review of Psychology, 65,* 209–233.

7 Weiss, R. S. (2005). *The experience of retirement.* New York, NY: Cornell University Press.

8 Moore, & Rosenthal. (2017). *Australian women in retirement survey.*
Hershey, D. A., & Henkens, K. (2013). Impact of different types of retirement transitions on perceived satisfaction with life. *The Gerontologist, 54,* 232–244.

9 Everingham, C., Warner-Smith, P., & Byles, J. (2007). Transforming retirement: Re-thinking models of retirement to accommodate the experiences of women. *Women's Studies International Forum, 30,* 512–522.

10 Schlossberg, N. (2004). *Retire smart, retire happy: Finding your true path in life.* Washington, DC: American Psychological Association.

11 Voltaire, Candide, Ch. 30.

12 Jahoda, M., Lazarsfeld, P., & Zeisel, H. (2002). *Marienthal: The sociography of an unemployed community.* Piscataway, NJ: Transaction Publishers.

13 *Retirement: A full-time job.* Retrieved from http://retiredsyd.typepad.com/retirement_a_fulltime_job/2013/05/finding-a-new-identity-in-retirement.html

CHAPTER 2

1 Cussen, M. P. (2017, March 16). Journey through the six stages of retirement. *Investopedia.* Retrieved from www.investopedia.com/articles/retirement/07/sixstages.asp

2 Kiso, H., & Hershey, D. A. (2017). Working adults' metacognitions regarding financial planning for retirement. *Work, Aging and Retirement, 3,* 77–88.

3 van den Bogaard, L. (2017). Leaving quietly? A quantitative study of retirement rituals and how they affect life satisfaction. *Work, Aging and Retirement, 3,* 55–65.

4 Price, C. A., & Nesteruk, O. (2015). What to expect when you retire: By women for women. *Marriage & Family Review, 51,* 418–440, p. 424.

5 Ibid, p. 425.

6 Erikson, E. H. (1963). *Childhood and society.* New York, NY: Norton.

7 Fisher, G. G., Chaffee, D. S., & Sonnega, A. (2016). Retirement timing: A review and recommendations for future research. *Work, Aging and Retirement, 2,* 230–261.

8 E.g., Warren, D. A. (2015). Retirement decisions of couples in Australia: The impact of spousal characteristics and preferences. *The Journal of the Economics of Ageing, 6,* 149–162.

9 Gustman, A. L., & Steinmeier, T. L. (2005). The social security early entitlement age in a structural model of retirement and wealth. *Journal of Public Economics*, 89, 441–463.

10 Lumsdaine, R. L., & Vermeer, S. J. C. (2015). Retirement timing of women and the role of care responsibilities for grandchildren. *Demography*, 52, 433–454.

CHAPTER 3

1 Quote from a participant in our research study. All other quotes are from our study participants unless noted otherwise.

2 Statistic Brain Research Institute. (2016). *Gender pay gap statistics*. CA, USA. Retrieved from https://www.statisticbrain.com/gender-pay-gap-statistics/

3 Economic Policy Institute. (2017). Retrieved from www.cnbc.com/2016/09/12/heres-how-much-the-average-american-family-has-saved-for-retirement.html

4 Express. (2017). Retrieved from www.express.co.uk/news/uk/782041/pension-warning-retirement-savings-britain-money-crisis

5 European Commission. (2015, April). *Database on women and men in decision-making*. Retrieved from ec.europa.eu/europe2020/pdf/ . . . /nrp2015_austria_annex1_1_en.pdf

6 U.S. Bureau of Labor Statistics. (2014). Retrieved from www.bls.gov/opub/mlr/2014/home.htm

7 Golladay, C. (2016). Schwab survey finds major differences in how male and female millennials view retirement. *Business Wire*, USA. Retrieved from www.businesswire.com/news/home/20161115005264/en/Schwab-Survey

8 Lusardi, A., & Mitchell, O. S. (2011). Financial literacy and retirement planning in the United States. *Journal of Pension Economics and Finance*, 10, 509–525.

9 The correct answers are (1) More than $102; (2) Less than today; (3) False.

10 Global Financial Literary Excellence Center (GFLEC). (2017). *Women and financial literacy: OECD/INFE evidence, survey and policy responses report*. Russia Financial Literacy and Education Trust Fund, George Washington University, Washington, DC.

11 Bucher-Koenen, T., Lusardi, A., Alessie, R. J. M., & van Rooij, M. C. J. (2016, February). *How financially literate are women? An overview and new insights*. Working Paper 2016–1, Global Financial Literary Excellence Center (GFLEC).

12 Richard Denniss, Chief Economist and former Executive Director, The Australia Institute.

13 OECD. (2017). *Pension policy notes and reviews*. Retrieved from www.oecd.org/pensions/policy-notes-and-reviews.htm

CHAPTER 4

1 World Health Organisation. (2011). *Global health and aging*. Bethesda, MD: WHO.

2 Hessel, P. (2016). Does retirement (really) lead to worse health among European men and women across all educational levels? *Social Science & Medicine, 151*, 19–26.

3 Eibich, P. (2015). Understanding the effect of retirement on health: Mechanisms and heterogeneity. *Journal of Health Economics, 43*, 1–12.

4 Holt-Lunstad, J., Smith, T. B., & Layton, J. B. (2010). Social relationships and mortality risk: A meta-analytic review. *PLoS Medicine, 7(7)*, Article ID: e1000316.

5 Zhu, R. (2016). Retirement and its consequences for women's health in Australia. *Social Science & Medicine, 163*, 117–125.

6 Helldán, A., Lallukka, T., Rahkonen, O., & Lahelma, E. (2012). Changes in healthy food habits after transition to old age retirement. *European Journal of Public Health, 22*, 582–586.

7 Dave, D., Rashad, I., & Spasojevic, J. (2008). The effects of retirement on physical and mental health outcomes. *Southern Economic Journal, 75*, 497–523.

8 Heybroek, L., Haynes, M., & Baxter, J. (2015). Life satisfaction and retirement in Australia: A longitudinal approach. *Work, Aging and Retirement, 1*, 166–180.

9 Sahlgren, G. H. (2013). *Work longer, live*. IEA Discussion Paper No. 46, Institute of Economic Affairs, UK.

10 Barbosa, L. M., Monteiro, L., & Giardini Murta, S. (2016). Retirement adjustment predictors: A systematic review. *Work, Aging and Retirement, 2*, 262–280.

11 Ibid.

12 Bamburger, P. A. (2015). Winding down and boozing up: The complex link between retirement and alcohol misuse. *Work, Aging and Retirement, 1*, 92–111.

13 Holdsworth, L., Hing, N., & Breen, H. (2012). Exploring women's problem gambling: A review of the literature. *International Gambling Studies, 12*, 199–213.

14 Sjosten, N. M., Kivimaki, M., Singh-Manoux, A., & Vahtera, J. (2012). Change in physical activity and weight in relation to retirement: The French GAZEL Cohort Study. *BMJ Open, 21*.

15 Duberley, J., Carmichael, F., & Szmigin, I. (2014). Exploring women's retirement: Continuity, context and career transition. *Gender, Work and Organization, 21*, 71–90.

CHAPTER 5

1 Tambourini, C. R. (2007). The never-married in old age: Projections and concerns for the near future. *Social Security Bulletin*, 67, 25–40.

2 Patulny, R. (2009). The golden years? Social isolation among retired men and women in Australia. *Family Matters*, 83, 39–47, Australian Institute of Family Studies.

3 Damman, M., & van Duijn, R. (2017). Intergenerational support in the transition from work to retirement. *Work, Aging and Retirement*, 3(1), 66–76.

4 Rosenthal, D. A., & Moore, S. M. (2012). *New age nanas: Being a grandmother in the 21st century*. Newport, NSW, Australia: Big Sky Publishing, pp. 79–80.

5 Ibid;

Moore, S. M., & Rosenthal, D. A. (2016). *Grandparenting: Contemporary perspectives*. London: Taylor and Francis;

Moore, S. M., & Rosenthal, D. A. (2014). Personal growth, grandmother engagement and satisfaction among non-custodial grandmothers. *Aging and Mental Health*, 19, 136–143.

6 For example, Thiele, D. M., & Whelan, T. A. (2008). The relationship between grandparent satisfaction, meaning and generativity. *International Journal of Aging and Human Development*, 66(1), 21–48;

The Berlin aging study. Retrieved from www.base-berlin.mpg.de/en (Study finds grandparents who babysit live longer).

7 Grigoryeva, A. (2014). *When gender trumps everything: The division of parent care among siblings*. American Sociological Association's 109th Annual Meeting, San Francisco.

8 Social Security Office of Retirement Policy (USA). (undated). *Population profiles*. Retrieved from www.ssa.gov/retirementpolicy/fact-sheets/marital-status-poverty.html;

Tamborini. (2007). The never-married in old age: Projections and concerns for the near future. *Social Security Bulletin*, 67(2), 25–40.

9 Kendig, H., Gong, C. H., Cannon, L., & Browning, C. (2017). Preferences and predictors of aging in place: Longitudinal evidence from Melbourne, Australia. *Journal of Housing for the Elderly*, 31(3), 259–271.

10 Patulny (2009). The golden years? Social isolation among retired men and women in Australia. *Family Matters*, 83.

11 Eisenberg, R. (2016). *Retirement life: Men and women do it very differently*. Retrieved from www.forbes.com/sites/nextavenue/2016/04/20/retirement-life-women-and-men-do-it-very-differently/#4eb395bb3dd8.

12 Dixon, G. (2017). *What lonely over-60s miss the most*. Retrieved from www.oversixty. com.au/health/caring/2017/01/what-lonely-over-60s-miss-the-most/

13 Hawkley, L. C., Hughes, M. E., Waite, L. J., Masi, C. M., Thisted, R. A., & Cacioppo, J. T. (2008). From social structural factors to perceptions of relationship quality and loneliness: The Chicago Health, Aging, and Social Relations Study. *The Journals of Gerontology Series B: Psychological Sciences and Social Sciences*, 63(6), S375–S384;

   Hawkley, L. C., & Cacioppo, J. T. (2007). Aging and loneliness. *Current Directions in Psychological Science*, 16(4), 187–191.

14 Holt-Lunstad, J., Smith, T. B., & Layton, J. B. (2010). Social relationships and mortality risk: A meta-analytic review. *PLoS Medicine*, 7(7), Article ID: e1000316.

15 Steptoe, A., Shankar, A., Demakakos, P., & Wardle, J. (2013). Social isolation, loneliness, and all-cause mortality in older men and women. *Proceedings of the National Academy of Sciences of the United States of America (PNAS)*, 110(15), 5797–5801.

16 Steffens, N. K., Cruwys, T., Haslam, C., Jetten, J., & Haslam, S. A. (2016). Social group memberships in retirement are associated with reduced risk of premature death: Evidence from a longitudinal cohort study. *BMJ Open*, 6, e010164.

17 Steptoe et al. (2013). Social isolation, loneliness, and all-cause mortality in older men and women. *Proceedings of the National Academy of Sciences of the United States of America*, 110, 5797–5801.

18 Greenfield, E. A., & Marks, N. F. (2004). Formal volunteering as a protective factor for older adults' psychological well being. *Journal of Gerontology: Social Sciences*, 59B, S258–S264.

19 Steptoe et al. (2013). Social isolation, loneliness, and all-cause mortality in older men and women. *Proceedings of the National Academy of Sciences of the United States of America*, 110, 5797–5801.

20 For example: Stanley, I. H., Conwell, Y., Bowen, C., & Van Orden, K. A. (2014). Pet ownership may attenuate loneliness among older adult primary care patients who live alone. *Aging and Mental Health*, 18, 394–399.

CHAPTER 6

1 Wang, M., & Shi, J. (2014). Psychological research on retirement. *Annual Review of Psychology*, 65, 209–233;

   Reitzes, D. C., & Mutran, E. J. (2004). The transition to retirement: Stages and factors that influence retirement adjustment. *International Journal of Aging and Human Development*, 59, 63–84;

Reitzes, D. C., Mutran, E. J., & Fernandez, M. E. (1996). Preretirement influences on postretirement self-esteem. *Journal of Gerontology: Social Sciences, 51B,* S242–S249;

Reitzes, D. C., & Mutran, E. J. (2006). Lingering identities in retirement. *The Sociological Quarterly, 47,* 333–359.

2 Ibid.

3 Topa, G., & Alcover, C. (2015). Psychosocial factors in retirement intentions and adjustment: A multi-sample study. *Career Development International, 20,* 384–408.

4 Ibid;

Zaniboni, S., Sarchielli, G., & Fraccaroli, F. (2010). How are psychosocial factors related to retirement intentions? *International Journal of Manpower, 31,* 271–285.

5 Barnes, H., & Parry, J. (2004). Renegotiating identity and relationships: Men and women's adjustments to retirement. *Ageing and Society, 24,* 213–233, p. 24.

6 Ibid.

7 Herron, A. (2017). *Male engineers extending working life: Issues in ongoing professional practice development.* PhD thesis, Faculty of Business and Law, Swinburne University of Technology, Australia. Retrieved from https://researchbank.swinburne.edu.au/file/2df8798a-58c1-4c20-acf9-e38361ab2d24/1/Alison%20Herron%20Thesis.pdf

8 Price, C. A. (2003). Professional women's retirement adjustment: The experience of reestablishing order. *Journal of Aging Studies, 17,* 341–355.

9 Ibid, p. 348.

10 Borrero, L., & Kruger, T. M. (2015). The nature and meaning of identity in retired professional women. *Journal of Women and Aging, 27,* 309–329.

11 Reitzes & Mutran. (2006). Lingering identities in retirement, p. 354.

12 Teuscher, U. (2010). Change and persistence of personal identities after the transition to retirement. *International Journal of Aging and Human Development, 70,* 89–106.

13 Moore, S. M., & Rosenthal, D. A. (2017). *Australian women in retirement survey.* Final Research Report. Unpublished document available from the authors.

CHAPTER 7

1 Friedan, B. (1993). *The fountain of age.* New York, NY: Simon and Schuster.

2 Karpen, R. R. (2017). Reflections on women's retirement. *Gerontologist, 57,* 103–109, p. 108.

3 Earl, J. K., Gerrans, P., & Halim, V. A. (2015). Active and adjusted: Investigating the contribution of leisure, health and psychosocial factors to retirement adjustment. *Leisure Sciences*, 37, 354–372.

4 Jaumont-Pascual, N., Monteagudo, M. J., Kleiber, D. A., & Cuenca, J. (2016). Gender differences in meaningful leisure following major later life events. *Journal of Leisure Research*, 48, 83–103.

5 Earl, J. (2017). *Engaging employees in retirement planning makes business sense*. Retrieved from indaily.com.au

6 See *Dr Happy's tips for positive thinking*. Retrieved from www.drhappy.com.au

7 Edgar, P., & Edgar, D. (2017). *Peak: Reinventing middle age*. Melbourne, Australia: Text Publishing Co.

8 Ibid., p. 92

9 Rosenthal, D. A., & Moore, S. M. (2012). *New age nanas: Being a grandmother in the 21st century*. Newport, NSW, Australia: Big Sky Publishing, pp. 79–80.

10 Your Life Choices. (2017, September 29). *George Carlin talks 'getting old'*. Retrieved from yourlifechoices.com.au